THE DO-IT-YOURSELF GUIDE TO Conscious Living

UNRAVELING YOUR MINDSETS IN 21 DAYS

By Lorie Givens

In no way is this book intended as a substitute for the medical advice of physicians or mental health professionals. It is recommended that readers regularly consult physicians or healthcare professionals in matters relating to their health and particularly with respect to any symptoms that may require diagnosis or medical attention.

Print ISBN: 978-17326890-0-8
eBook ISBN: 978-1-7326890-1-5

Book cover and interior design by
Tara Mayberry, TeaBerryCreative.com

"To believe your own thought, to believe that what is true for you in your private heart is true for all men—that is genius."

—RALPH WALDO EMERSON

Foreword

I once heard a religion professor say, "Often the best thing to do with advice is to ignore it." That particular advice has always been extremely easy for me to follow. And that's all those words are in the end—advice. No more, no less. Indeed advice that's easy to follow may not even feel like advice, but it still is. There is advice in this book. You wouldn't read it if it didn't have it, but it's advice that's easy to follow. In fact, after reading *The Do-It-Yourself Guide to Conscious Living*, you may not even realize you're following advice.

Lorie Givens is my older sister, and after reading this book, I wish I'd listened to her advice more often than I actually have. And the thing is, I usually do listen to her advice. In the past, when I've asked for her advice, Lorie usually suggests that I spend more time listening to myself and asking whether the criticisms inside my head were valid in any meaningful sense. Most importantly, she usually asks me if I'd say such criticism to a friend. If you are like me, you wouldn't spend much time with that voice, the one where everything is your fault and you're getting what you deserve. If this voice were another person, you'd block their number. You'd take the stairs rather than share an elevator. Sadly, this voice isn't another person. While this unkind voice represents a part of us, we're often convinced it's the most important part. When it comes to the advice it gives, such as *don't bother* or *you're no good*, we rarely ignore this advice, if ever. *The Do-It-Yourself Guide to Conscious Living* helps you manage this negative voice and ignore it altogether when necessary, and reading my sister's book taught me that.

Growing up as a child in the 70s and 80s, while it was obvious that weebles, pet rocks, and nerf balls were popular, it was less obvious how popular judging was. As far as my sister and I were concerned, virtually every adult authority figure we knew reinforced the importance of judging friends, neighbors, and most especially yourself. It was kind of what people did in those days, but in many respects, it's still what we do today. Although most systems of morality urge people to be humble, it can be awfully difficult to practice humility without excessively unkind self-judgment. For many people, it's hard enough to see these two as not being the very same thing. Writer Anne Lamott says that "we can change. People say we can't, but we do when the stakes or the pain is high enough." I agree with Lamott that all of us can change for the better. However, my sister demonstrates that it doesn't necessarily take pain to inspire change. It only takes 21 days and reading *The Do-It-Yourself Guide to Conscious Living.*

—Dr. Jerry Saviano,
Professor of English
University of Hawaii System

Introduction

WELCOME TO "THE DO-IT-YOURSELF GUIDE TO CONSCIOUS LIVING"

"Unraveling Your Mindsets in 21 Days"

This is a book built around a 21-day process where you'll be challenged, motivated, possibly even persuaded to start paying attention to not only what you think but to how what you think affects you. Much of what you'll discover in the process are ways of thinking you've owned most of your life, many of which you likely never thought of as ways of thinking and, even less likely, your ownership of them. That's why it's titled a "Do-it-Yourself" guide. It is self-help in its purest form. Not only does it start with the self but it also ends with the self. All I did was condense it to make it easier for you and present it in such a way that, hopefully, will make you think and want to pay attention. Be forewarned though: some of what you read and hear may feel a bit uncomfortable at times. I didn't write a book about how to feel good or how to tell people what they want to hear. In my opinion, there already are far too many books and people telling us what we want to hear, and far too few nudging us to look at ourselves a little differently. But I promise you that "The Do-It-Yourself Guide to Conscious Living" will not only inspire you to look at yourself a little differently, but it will also help you understand your role in whatever it is that you see.

This book is not a personal memoir. It does not focus on me or my mostly unremarkable life story. Instead, it focuses on something far more remarkable which is how much we all share in terms of our lack of self-awareness. We all constantly talk to ourselves, yet we almost never pay attention to the fact that we do. There are close to seven and a half billion people living on the planet, and we all spend most of our lives in conversation with ourselves! In our heads! And we seldom even think about it. So perhaps this book is a collective memoir of our rather remarkable tendencies to live most of our lives engrossed in rather unremarkable discussions with ourselves without ever noticing the profound effects of those discussions. My book focuses on some of those effects while nudging you toward some of the insights you'll discover once you start paying attention to what you are telling yourself.

And it will be a discovery.

How do I know?

Because I went through my own process of unraveling my ways of thinking, and that's how I discovered how critical my role was in the process. Once I tuned in to what I was telling myself, I started uncovering mindsets inside of me that I never knew I had, and I began paying attention to how those mindsets were affecting my thoughts, my moods, and my mind. Quite surprisingly, I figured out that the most effective way to change my mind about one thing or another was to first change my mindset about it, but before I could do so, I had to figure out what my mindset actually was. So, since I was dealing with my mind, as well as my mindsets, I felt I needed to be front and center when it came to navigating my head. (Hence, the DIY revelation.) And that was the coolest part. I actually started watching how much time I spent thinking I was managing the busy world around me while overlooking how much more progress I could make by managing the even busier one inside me. Once I figured that out, the whole process started to make sense. I realized that not only did I need to step back to become the observer in my life, but I also needed to step forward to become the primary participant in my life. Now, having spent nearly four years doing so and writing about it, I am ready to show you how capable we are to act in both capacities.

Not only will this book encourage you to question and confront many of the ways you think and talk to yourself, but I'll be with you the whole time pointing out things you likely never noticed. I suspect you'll even forget that I'm there, but I guarantee that once you start looking at yourself a little more objectively, you'll start feeling more humility and civility, and you'll start appreciating how much more you have in common with everyone else.

And that, my friend, is how we will bring more civility to the planet. It's a matter of coming to recognize that civility is nothing more than a mindset or state of mind. It's just one that's become somewhat faded with lack of use.

Why I Wrote This Book

Although I didn't set out to write a self-help book, I did set out to help myself, and it occurred to me that quite often the things which help me the most are things I figure out on my own. In this case, I wanted to help myself become more aware, especially of me, and that included becoming more aware of not only *what* I was thinking but how it was affecting me. I guess you could say I wanted to live more consciously. One of the first things I discovered was that living consciously was not as easy as it sounded. It meant I needed to be aware of my thoughts which quickly showed me that most of my thoughts occur completely outside of my awareness. Naturally, I'm aware that I'm thinking, but I'm seldom aware of how that thinking is affecting me.

So I decided to write about it and then organize what I wrote into chapters. I began each chapter by asking myself why I thought the way I did about a variety of different things, and soon I realized that perhaps it was time for me to rethink a few things. This book reflects a lot of that rethinking. As a result, each chapter underwent multiple rewrites. In the earlier versions, I found myself picturing other people in my mind as I wrote, but it wasn't until I began picturing myself that the message hit its mark, and I began to connect the dots. So if, while reading or listening, you find yourself picturing other people, please give the chapter another go-round picturing yourself instead. I promise if you make an honest effort of it, the outcome will be very different the second time around.

Please note that I did not draw upon any formalized training or expertise in the field of self-help. I do not have that type of expertise or training. Instead, I drew upon hours and hours of contemplation, isolated reflection, as well as some occasional good old horse sense.

Looking back, perhaps that was the point: what I discovered was that it wasn't so much the training, formal or otherwise, that would be the key to living more consciously as it would be the re-training. In order to live more consciously, what I needed was to re-train myself, and that began with a realization that my ability to live more consciously would rest largely on my willingness to do so. In other words, in order for me to live more consciously, I had to commit to more conscious living. I had to commit to not only observing and paying attention to what I was thinking but also to figuring out how it was affecting me. In essence, I had to become aware of the relationship I was having with myself.

Having done so now for the greater part of four years, I am convinced, of all the relationships I have in life, the one that matters most is the one I have with me. Writing this book has helped me shift that relationship by shifting the conversations. And yes, just like you, I have conversations with myself. All the time. In my head. Just like you. Just like everyone.

See, these conversations, the ones we are having with ourselves, are what enable us to live consciously. It's really just a matter of waking up to them.

So maybe the work I've done to wake up to mine will inspire you to wake up to yours, and you'll find yourself living more consciously, too.

Author's Notes

This book is mostly about what we think, and not so much about why we think it or who, in particular, influenced us. I chose to leave more of the "why" and the "who" to the experts, so that you and I could focus on the "what" and, quite possibly, change the "how".

As you read or listen to the pages that follow, you'll often find me switching back and forth from talking to you to talking to myself, and that's exactly how I wrote it because that's how conversations in our heads tend to move along. You may also notice that several of the chapters overlap, and that was intentional, too. Although we have many different mindsets, the reasons behind them are often the same.

The book is organized into 21 chapters to be read over 21 days. I did this to encourage you to take your time with it but also to protect you from feeling pressured or rushed to get through it. If, however, you find yourself tempted to skip ahead, know that I thank you for your interest and eagerness, but I believe you will enjoy it much more if you take it one day at a time.

As I can tell you firsthand, getting accustomed to living consciously takes time. But it sure is worth it.

Contents

A will to succeed comes from a willingness.
We have to be willing to succeed in order to succeed.

Day One

A MINDSET OF SUCCESS

One and the Same

We want to be successful.

In fact, we want it so much that we constantly imagine ourselves being that way and how it would change our lives if we were.

But have we ever considered that maybe what's standing between us and being successful are the things we think we need to do in order to become successful?

Is it possible that we want to be a success a lot more than we want to become one, and if so, are we using the things we think we need to do in order to become successful as reasons not to succeed?

Maybe we just need to change our reasoning, which, if you think about it, shouldn't be that hard because we've been doing it our entire lives. It is how we've talked ourselves into and out of everything we've ever done. Everything. Whatever it was we did, we were front and center reasoning it to be, or changing our reasoning for it not to be. Whenever we were afraid, whenever we walked away, hesitated, or procrastinated, we reasoned our way through whatever we did. The reasoning may not have lasted more than a split second, but it took place, and it came from us, even if it only came through as images in our minds. Whichever way it happened though, we used it to stall our success or, at least, to stall the process we had decided preceded success, which was the same process we had decided was required for becoming successful.

And most of our reasoning was based on how we had imagined ourselves becoming, or not becoming, successful.

Oddly enough, these were the same imaginations we had used as kids to be whatever we wanted, and a lot of what we wanted was to be superheroes. So we willed it to be, and superheroes were what we became. We donned our capes, faced our foes and prevailed. We filled our minds with thoughts of power, and the more we filled, the more powerful we became. Then we used our powers to ensure our success every single time. Somehow, as kids, we knew that in order to be a superhero, each day we would need to demonstrate our unique powers and superhuman strength. So to fulfill these demonstrations, each day our imaginations would bring forth a new villain or, at least, a new threat that would challenge our success. We never were deterred by these challenges though, because we knew the only way we could retain our superhero status was by re-earning it through each new mission, and we were ready, willing and eager every single day to re-earn superhero status. We knew you couldn't just *be* a superhero. Every day you had to become one.

That's what being a superhero meant! So every day we set out to prove it, mostly to ourselves, or maybe to our friends who also were superheroes. Day after day we called on all our skills and proved that nothing could defeat us. As far as we were concerned, we were unstoppable. We willed ourselves to be powerful and we believed in our own power. It never occurred to us that there was any difference between our reality and our imaginations.

Nor did it occur to us that lots of people in our lives would soon focus on convincing us otherwise. See, those people had also been convinced otherwise. They had learned that growing up meant they no longer could live in their worlds of make-believe. So it was incumbent on them to help us grow up and to show us that the things we were imagining weren't real. We had to learn how to separate fact from fiction; facts were cold and hard, but supposedly necessary in order for us to get serious. This business of getting serious was important, even though it wasn't completely clear to us what "serious" was. We just knew that no one laughed or smiled when they said it, and it made us feel like we were being tied down. The consensus was that, by getting serious, we would learn our place in the world. We also would learn how to live within tight schedules and deadlines—the kind of deadlines which left little time for imagining. The consensus also seemed to agree that imagining wasn't productive enough, even though our imaginations had always left us feeling very productive. In fact, our early childhood feelings of productivity were what fueled our insatiable desire to produce more. No wonder we always felt so full of energy, so fearless and eager to explore! We didn't have time to waste sitting around separating the facts of who we were from the fiction of who we were because the two were one and the same.

That's one of the reasons we had so much energy—because they *were* one and the same! We believed we were powerful, and therefore, we were. It was that simple, and it was expressed through everything we did. We saw ourselves as successful, strong, and powerful. We felt it. We believed it, and as a result, constant power and energy surged throughout our little bodies and brains. Oh sure, every once in a while we would overhear comments about our "active imaginations and endless energy", but those comments usually fell pretty flat with us. They sounded almost meaningless because, as far as we could tell, there was nothing imaginary about how much we believed in ourselves, and there was nothing imaginary about the constant energy we felt that came from how much we believed in ourselves. Our beliefs were real. Our energy was real. And it all had come from one place: our minds.

The same minds we use today.

The same minds where the facts of who we believe we are still coincide with the fiction of who we believe we are. Except now, they don't leave us feeling quite as energized.

See, as kids, we started out using our minds, namely, our imaginations to make us believe we were powerful, but somewhere down the road, we began using them to make us believe we were powerless. The point is though, we never stopped using our imaginations; we just stopped using them to give us power. In many ways, we began using them to take power away from ourselves! Even though, as children, our imaginations had proven time after time how strong and capable they could make us feel, we began insisting that what we wanted to hear from them was the exact opposite. So we started changing what our imaginations told us. And even though it was still us, via our imaginations calling the shots, for some reason, we stopped referring to it as make-believe. But it still was. We still were imagining things that we made ourselves believe. That's what make-believe is: it's whatever we make ourselves believe. And usually, it's stuff we make up in our minds, and then we believe it. So really, we haven't changed how we make ourselves believe stuff; we've just changed the stuff we make up, but instead of recognizing that the stuff we're making up is causing us not to feel very good about ourselves, we make ourselves believe that we are using our skills of reasoning to play out various scenarios in our heads, even though many of those scenarios are completely imaginary, you know... fictional, made-up, not real. Of course, as grown-ups, we like to think that since we're imagining real people instead of fictional ones, the scenarios we're imagining are also real. But really, regardless of whether the people are real or fictional, we're still imagining, so this so-called reasoning we believe we're using doesn't seem all that reasonable. Nor does it seem, despite our training, that we really learned how to separate fact from fiction because, just like when we were kids, we still are blurring the lines between make-believe and reality, and we still are dreaming up lots and lots of imaginary scenarios we'll have to face in order to become successful. Except now, we are using those blurred lines as reasons not to become successful and not to power through whatever we're imagining stands between us and success. And just like when we were kids, we're accepting these fictional scenarios as fact without recognizing any of the striking parallels with our younger selves.

Nor do we recognize the distinctions. See, as kids, we mostly used our imaginations to power ourselves up! Yet as adults, we mostly use our imaginations to power ourselves down, and we rationalize our way through it by believing we've matured beyond the childish notions we held about ourselves. But here's what really happened, which, by the way, is quite contrary to what we generally associate with maturity: instead of allowing our belief in ourselves to mature alongside everything else that was maturing inside of us, we tucked away all that self-belief that had been so loyal to us throughout childhood, and we replaced it with self-doubt. Then we gave that growing sense of doubt so much power that by the time we were adults, it had become one of our most dominant beliefs. And by that time, why wouldn't we? We had crafted so many stories in our minds about our inabilities to succeed. We no longer believed in ourselves. We only believed in doubting ourselves. And there was nothing imaginary about how much we doubted ourselves. And there was nothing imaginary about the constant lack of energy we felt that came from how much we doubted ourselves. Our beliefs were real. Our lack of energy was real. We believed we were powerless, and therefore, we were.

Once again, it all had come from our minds.

- The same minds that never stopped to challenge how a belief system rooted in powerlessness could be mistaken for maturity!
- The same minds we had originally counted on to give us endless power and energy.
- The same minds that knew you couldn't just *be* a success any more than you could just *be* a superhero!

Because the heroics come from becoming one.

- The heroics come from knowing we're going to face challenges and facing them anyway.
- They come from appreciating that success is a process, not just an outcome, because most of the energy that comes from success, comes from the process that *leads* to success.
- Success is not a state of being; it's a set of feelings we develop along the way.
- So if we really want success, and we really want to change the course of our lives, all we really need to change is the course of our imaginations.
- Because the facts of who we believe we are will constantly align with the fiction of who we believe we are.
- Our beliefs are what make them one and the same.

If you occasionally offer your ear to others, don't be surprised when they rise to the occasion.

Day Two

A MINDSET OF LISTENING

Who We Have in Mind

Have you ever noticed how drawn you are to someone who takes a genuine interest in what you have to say? Someone who actually pays attention, maybe even asks questions and then sticks around for whatever you say next?

Although we often credit shared interests and compatibilities as the backbones of our friendships, how many of those friendships came about because someone gave us their attention? They stopped and listened, and their simple act of listening gave us that special feeling that whatever it was we said was heard and, for however long it lasted, it mattered.

Despite how much it matters though, as well as how much can come from it, this simple act is rather rare, so maybe it's not as simple as we think.

Maybe that's because listening means we have to slow down our thoughts long enough to make room for someone else's. We have to offer them the same courtesy we would offer another driver trying to merge onto a busy superhighway; we have to make a conscious decision to let them go ahead of us.

Listening is a conscious decision, too; it's just one we often don't like making because it requires us to put someone else's desire to be heard above our own, and doing so feels almost unnatural, at times. So, we compromise by listening with ourselves in mind. Albeit unknowingly, we make listening about us. We take what someone else is saying and convert it into what we think they're meaning while simultaneously paying attention to other ideas and distractions we find more interesting or compelling. When it comes to listening, we're constantly choosing between paying attention to someone else's thoughts and our own. Of course, at times, we know we're making these choices, but we rarely consider how these choices are affecting our own tendencies and preferences toward listening. Although we may think we're good listeners, we're seldom as good as we think once we start paying attention to how we listen.

If you don't believe it, start paying attention to how you listen. Watch how frequently you feel an urge to interject, change the subject, give advice, talk about yourself, or disengage. Notice how you constantly switch back and forth from what someone else is saying to what you're thinking. Compare how many times you feel distracted to how many times you give in to those distractions.

Perhaps more importantly though, watch how other people respond to how you listen. Are they competing with you to get their message across or relaxing into an easiness you've created for them? Are they sharing more or less with you as a result?

Now picture yourself and how *you* feel when someone listens to you the way you listen to others.

Maybe in order to change how people listen to us, we need to change how we listen to them. Maybe listening with a little more selfless intent will encourage others to respond in kind. Perhaps the way we've been listening has robbed us of some of the closer connections we long for.

Since there were so few people in our lives who had shown us how to listen more consciously though, we likely had no idea we had made it about us and, for the same reason, neither had they. So in order to be heard, we all turned our attention inward and began a habit of listening to ourselves. Of course, we didn't do it knowingly; nor did we feel absorbed in our own thoughts. There were so many demands on our time and so many other things we needed and wanted to think about that we had no choice but to postpone listening to other people until there was more time. We all know that listening requires time, particularly the kind we don't think we have, so it's hard to make time for things that demand more from us than we're able, or even willing, to give. Listening demands we give of ourselves or, at least, that's how it feels, especially when we give to those who give sparingly in return. As a result, some of our give-and-take relationships leave us feeling a bit taken and uninspired to find time we really don't want to look for in the first place. So, we either turn to others, or we turn inward.

The point is though that we're turning somewhere hoping to be heard which often means turning to ourselves because no one else is listening, and the reason they're not is because they're listening to themselves, too.

We're all so busy listening to ourselves that we're not hearing each other. No wonder the connections between us often feel strained and disconnected. Without even knowing it, we've made listening about us, and since most everyone else has, too, we've created an almost universal paradox where everyone wants to be heard, but almost no one wants to listen.

We all are fighting to be heard.

And with so many of us engaged in the same fight at the same time for the same reason, we all end up sounding pretty much the same.

We sound like noise.

Perhaps we've placed so much emphasis on being heard that we've stopped listening to anything other than what we want to hear by tuning in what we like and tuning out what we don't, but if everyone does this, how will we ever hear what each other is saying or, at least, trying to say? Will we just keep fighting to be heard to the point that none of us are listening to anything other than the chatter in our own minds? Must we lose our senses of hearing in order to realize the vital roles they play in our relationships, including the breakdowns which result when we don't use them?

Is doing without the only way to fully appreciate how much easier "doing with" really is?

Couldn't we all do with a few better listeners in our lives? Is it possible those listeners are already there, and we just haven't noticed each other because we've all been paying too much attention to ourselves?

It's an easy fix though since the only thing that listening really requires is consciously putting our minds somewhere and then, keeping them there. Giving one another our undivided attention will help us feel less divided. We can start gaining or even regaining each other's trust because listening, especially when it's done in earnest, moves us toward trust.

If we just approach it differently, we can come to see listening for the act of charity it really is: giving something freely without expecting anything in return. It's only when we make listening about us that it begins to lose its charitability. When we give of ourselves, especially when we do it charitably, we get to walk away from the experience knowing we gave without looking to get. See, the selfless things we do to make others feel better about themselves are the very things that make us feel better about ourselves. In other words, helping other people feel like they matter makes us feel like we matter, too. And when more people feel like they matter, they're a lot less focused on conflict, division, and self-interest.

Listening brings us together and makes us feel connected. It's only when we don't listen that those connections start to unravel.

Granted, we all have people in our lives who never seem to listen, who constantly interrupt, maybe even talk over us, and yes, as a result, we may have gotten used to tuning them out, almost entirely. But it's possible that other people have tuned us out for the same reasons.

Maybe we all could use a bit more charity, and maybe we really can change how people listen to us by changing how we listen to them. How will we know if we never try?

Perhaps it's time we paid attention to paying attention.

It's time we realized that listening is mostly about who we have in mind.

Our worlds are only full of opposition when we polarize what we see.

Day Three

A MINDSET OF PRAISE AND CRITICISM

What's Your Ratio?

We notice something we really like or admire about someone else, but how often do we tell them? How often do we take the praise that we're thinking or feeling about someone else and convert it to praise that we're giving someone else? Since we generally refer to it as "giving praise", how often do we think of it as a gift? It certainly feels like a gift when praise is being given to us. It's one of those feelings we hope will last far longer than it usually does, and it often takes us to one of those feel-good places we go back to later and replay in our heads. Even if we feel a bit clumsy or awkward in how we receive it, or we act mostly unfazed by having received it, there's no denying it feels good, especially if it's the kind of praise that leaves us feeling special, even valued. And for however long it lasts or however long we allow it to last, we look at ourselves a little differently. We see ourselves through the words of praise that someone else gives us, and our day takes a bit of an upward turn because they took the time to tell us.

Of course, most of the time we don't think about what may have gone on inside of them in order for them to give us the praise; that's because we're so focused on the praise and on feeling all the good feelings that come with receiving it. We're seldom aware though, that any focus is involved. If anything, we're just aware that it feels good, even if we're not aware that it mostly feels good because we keep thinking about it, which is generally what makes most things feel good. It's also what makes most things feel better, and provided we keep thinking those same kinds of things, the better it feels.

In other words, whenever we receive praise, how long it lasts and what effect it has depends on us. Criticism works that way, too. Whenever we receive criticism, how long it lasts and what effect it has also depends us. So, if criticism and praise work pretty much the same way in terms of how we receive them, why is it we often allow criticism to have a much greater effect? Is it because we give and receive so much more of it?

Whether we're doing it in our heads or doing it with one another, we are constantly pointing out what's wrong and making note of all the little things in life we don't much care for. By doing so, most of us have gotten really good at calling attention and then paying attention to whatever we think is bad. You might even say that we're really good at figuring out what's bad. In fact, we even praise ourselves for being great critics and having discriminating taste which, in layman's terms, means we feel rather special for having developed a long list of things we don't like and a much shorter list of things we do. Of course, many of us may not think of our own taste as being very discriminating, but chances are we go about our days as amateur critics spending far more time criticizing things we don't like vs. praising things we do. And since most everyone we know approaches criticism in pretty much the same way, we seldom even notice. Nor do we notice that, by getting so comfortable criticizing, the comfort makes it no longer feel like criticism. It just feels like us.

So how can we expect that others who are so much like us, especially in this regard, feel anything other than comfort when they criticize? And with so many people feeling so much comfort with so much criticism, is it any wonder that who we usually end up criticizing is each other?

We've gotten so comfortable criticizing each other, and that comfort comes mostly from having done so much criticizing. So naturally, by having done so much of it, we've become much quicker to criticize while becoming more reluctant to praise. In essence, we've trained ourselves to look for the bad, and that training has convinced us there's more "bad" to be seen. By the same token, we've trained ourselves not to look for the good, and that training has convinced us there's less good to be seen. Since we've trained ourselves to see more bad than good, that's what we look for, and if that's what we look for, then that's what we see. Maybe we didn't intend to do so, but we've also trained ourselves to separate what we see into bad vs. good, yes vs. no, agree vs. disagree, or like vs. dislike, but the funny part is that we were the ones who created or, at least, came to believe in all these opposites and then trained ourselves to look for them. A real duality of sorts.

Perhaps some part of us believes that in order to appreciate the good, we must experience the bad, or in order to feel happiness, we must have known sadness. Or, in order to value praise, we must have been devalued by criticism. But at some point in time, perhaps years ago, the part of us that came to believe such things learned to do so; we just may not have been aware we were learning. Maybe it would be more accurate to say we just weren't aware we were being trained, and that training included praise for behavior which was considered good and criticism for behavior which was considered not good. It was this kind of training which inspired in us an inclination toward dividing things into opposites, as well as a habit of viewing things as opposed and, of course, after living so many years thinking in these terms, we almost never recognize that we do. But we do, and maybe if we became more aware that we do, we'd begin to understand that a habit of viewing things as opposed eventually causes us to interpret or expect things to be in opposition to *us*. See, this internal feeling of opposition is what feeds our desire to criticize, and that's why we criticize far more often than we praise.

In essence, we've filled ourselves with opposition by polarizing what we see.

So maybe if we start paying attention to our own inclinations toward criticism and opposition, we'll begin noticing more of the praise-worthy things which previously slipped past our gaze. Those praise-worthy things are happening all around us. We just haven't noticed them because of what's been happening inside of us.

But a little conscious effort can change all of that. If we stop looking for polarity and dwelling in opposition, we'll start feeling much less inclined to criticize. We may even feel more inclined to share some of the praise we previously would have offered only sparingly because we felt less comfortable doing so. But offering praise, especially when it's done sincerely, without pretense or without an expectation for something in return, often leads to some very nice feelings not only for the receiver, but the giver, too.

Praise really is a gift. At times its value is just as great for the giver as it is for the receiver. And we know this because of how good we feel when we give it or receive it.

How many relationships could we mend if we chose to offer a small amount of praise instead of our more generous amount of criticism? Wouldn't we eventually reach a more satisfying criticism to praise ratio?

Kind of makes you wonder: what's your ratio?

Putting people down is easy. It's lifting them up that really shows what we're made of.

Day Four

A MINDSET OF PASSING JUDGMENT

What is the Rush?

Whether we stand in it, pass it, or rush to it, the act of judgment, especially of others, comes as naturally to us as breathing.

But make us the subject of judgment, especially by others, and watch us squirm.

So, why is it that judging others feels so natural, but being judged by others feels so unnatural? Like two sides of the same coin.

We spend so much of our lives rushing to judgment about everything and everyone. Yet despite all this rushing, we often forget that others are rushing, too.

- » We all are rushing to judgment.
- » It's just what we do.
- » We do it all the time.
- » We do it quickly and efficiently.

And much of the time, we have absolutely no idea we are doing it.

Of course, almost every judgment we make starts out as an observation, but we almost never allow them to remain as observations. In fact, it's pretty tough to pinpoint when an observation becomes a judgment. We're so efficient with the process that we seldom notice there is one.

Since our observations need meaning, we compare and contrast them with other things we've given meaning by categorizing, ranking and labeling them. Everything needs a label, and according to the way we operate, almost every person needs one, too. So, we give them one. Frequently, more than one. Overall, we're pretty generous when it comes to handing out labels. Maybe that's because labels help us legitimize things. They also help us familiarize ourselves with the unfamiliar. So most things don't stay unfamiliar very long because once we observe them, pass judgment, assign a few labels, and then place them in a category, we start relying on those judgments, even though they may be brand new with only a few seconds separating them from our observations.

Of course, if you time us, it may seem like we are rushing, but if you ask us, we'll probably defend our quickness. We might even say that "rushing to judgment" doesn't feel like rushing, at all. It doesn't evoke any of the feelings we normally associate with hurrying. Maybe it does appear to be happening on the fly, but since we've spent our whole lives making judgments that way, it would feel almost counter-intuitive to slow down. So perhaps, the efficiencies we've developed in our efforts to make sense of the world have, in turn, led us to making rather hasty judgments, including the ones we make about each other.

We often and openly display this hastiness when it comes to judging our family members and friends. Maybe that's because we feel so vested in these judgments, or we see ourselves as subject matter experts, often claiming to know our loved ones better than they know themselves.

But do we really? Know them better than they know themselves? Or is it more likely that what we know, or what we think we know, are mostly judgments we've made about them? Oftentimes these judgments end up influencing their behavior or, at least, their behavior around us. Occasionally our judgments affect them so much that they alter the judgments they make about themselves, which, by the way, gives us a good bit of validation, as well as that "told you so" kind of confirmation we often use to pass more judgments and feel more familiar with whomever we're judging.

Somehow, the more familiar we become *with* one another, the more relaxed we become passing judgment *about* one another. Familiarity tends to have that effect on us, or maybe we tend to have that effect on familiarity.

Also, the more judgments we pass, the more narrowly focused our judgments tend to become, which ends up narrowing the spaces into which we expect others to fit, sort of like continually expecting someone to squeeze into a smaller pair of already too-tight jeans. In our defense though, we're not always aware that our judgments are becoming narrower because much of the time we're not even aware that we are judging.

Of course, if someone else happens to be listening to or watching us, it's not hard for them to figure out that we're passing judgment, especially the narrowing sort which tends to sound more like criticisms. As judgments tend to beget more judgments, so do criticisms tend to beget more criticisms; and the more we criticize, the more we use judgments to find fault, especially when it comes to finding fault with each other.

So whether it's our familiarity with one another or our familiarity with criticism, familiarity does breed contempt, just like the saying goes. But the saying doesn't mention that we are the breeders. Yes, familiarity may help us be better breeders, but we don't need familiarity in order to feel contempt. We can, and often do, feel contempt for people we barely know, people we don't know, people we only know of, or even people we are seeing for the very first time. And if what we see or feel strikes a familiar chord of contempt inside of us, we end up making judgments about people which, at times, are hard for us to un-make. Maybe to some degree that's because we use a rather innocuous label to categorize these judgments. We call them "impressions", and we like to think of them as marks or imprints that others leave behind as if our role in the formation of these judgments is mostly passive. Clearly, the judgments are ours, but perhaps, because we believe that other people are shaping them, we often end up allowing *first* impressions to become *lasting* ones.

So, despite how much we may think our roles are separate or disconnected to the making of these impressions, our judgments are busy deciding what they mean. Impressions don't have meaning until we give them meaning, and they don't make imprints until we allow them to. How deeply an imprint is made is also decided through our judgments, because our judgments are decisions. They are our decisions. Every time we pass judgment, we make a decision. We decide to evaluate something or someone in a particular way and, more often than not, we do so in order to satisfy a particular feeling we're wanting, expecting, or are accustomed to feeling. Naturally, the more we feel these feelings, the more we rely on our decisions, namely, these judgments that we've made. It all happens within fractions of seconds outside of our awareness. We pass judgment to satisfy or confirm one of our feelings, and then we move on to the next judgment.

One of the feelings we generally are seeking to satisfy is one that makes us feel better about ourselves. Our judgments tend to be very self-sustaining in this regard which might be why we rely on them so much. Our desire to feel better about ourselves plays a huge part in how we construct many of our judgments, especially ones about others. See, if we can see limitations in others, then we won't feel quite so bad about the ones we see in ourselves. So, especially when it comes to others, we look for limitations or, at least, what we decide are limitations. And with all the practice we have looking for limitations, we almost always find them, even if it means we have to manufacture them in our minds. As soon as we can pinpoint what we think is a limitation, we can get back to business as usual. We can assign or attach a new label that fits the limitation we think we see, and then we can place whomever we're judging into one of our nicely sorted categories. Once we place them into a category, we can get used to viewing them through the limitations of that category.

Granted, as time goes on, we may shuffle around our categories here and there to include additional limitations we've found, but more often than not, we prefer to look at people through a singular lens, even though we forget that we are the ones giving the lens its shape.

In other words, we see limitations in others because that's what we want to see. If we want to see that someone lacks or possesses a certain quality, our minds will give us exactly what we want, because our minds take whatever our eyes are seeing and our ears are hearing, and then filter it through our own assumptions, opinions, and expectations. Since we're so accustomed to this constant filtering, most of the time we forget that it's occurring. We may even forget that we are involved. And all the while, we're rushing to judgment and quite possibly, jumping to conclusions because of what we want to see. But most of the time, we have no idea that what we want has anything to do with it. And that's pretty much what happens when we set out to look for limitations in others. All too often though, we end up limiting ourselves to rather narrowly-focused judgments: the same judgments which end up limiting us from making good judgments.

Perhaps, we could summarize by saying that the primary reason we have difficulty seeing people for who and what they are is because we are so caught up in seeing them for who and what we want them to be.

So, regardless of how multi-dimensional people may actually be or have the potential to be, we often and unknowingly compress them into an intangibly smaller space of what we want them to be. Doing so makes us feel as if they now have less potential for eclipsing us, because the smaller everyone else becomes in our minds, the less complex and enigmatic they seem, and the less threatened we feel. It's almost as if we are constantly trying to shrink one another. If we can compartmentalize one another into a shrunken set of variables, we can make our individual worlds feel safer, more organized, more manageable and predictable.

But we surely do underestimate one another in the process.

And we participate in the same system when it comes to us because everyone else is trying to put us into their categories. They're trying to make us fit into their smaller spaces, just like we do to them. If they don't think we fit very well into one group, they mentally transfer us into another group. And so on and so on. At times it feels as if you almost can see the wheels turning inside someone else's head as they "feel you out" and "size you up". The unfortunate result though is that a lot of the time we buy into the categories where others place us. Even if we did nothing to contribute to the placement, or even if the category feels completely alien to us, we often react by looking at ourselves through the judgments that other people make about us. Of course, sometimes we get pretty defensive about it, but the main reason we tend to get defensive is because we worry their judgments might be true. We start second-guessing ourselves, and the result is we start feeling small.

Small enough to fit into someone else's category.

Then we start running through the mental checklists of what we did wrong, or how did we misstep or why are we unappealing? Once we start running in this direction, it's hard to slow down. And it all comes from self-doubt. The ironic thing though, about *self*-doubt is that much of it originated outside of us, as doubt handed to us from someone else. It only became self-doubt because we let it get inside of us. Then we gave it momentum, legitimized it, and made it real.

Sound familiar?

We took someone else's judgment of us, and then we used it to stand in judgment of ourselves.

And we surely did underestimate ourselves in the process.

See, passing judgment leads to a lot of underestimation.

It also leads to inaccuracies, lost opportunities, and extinguished potential.

So maybe the next time we catch ourselves on the cusp of a judgment we're rushing to pass, a label we're trying to assign, or a characteristic we're trying to categorize, we could pause to consider if the sense we are trying to make of the world really makes sense. Or would it make more sense to consider that we could be chasing a familiar feeling we want to feel? Because our habit of rushing to judgment, particularly with negative or destructive judgments, has too often led us to making misjudgments, and those misjudgments have mostly limited us.

Why have we been in such a hurry to pass judgment, to form opinions and to underestimate ourselves and other people?

Perhaps it's time we chose a different pace, and perhaps it's time to consider that when it comes to something as important as standing in judgment, what *is* the rush?

Self-serving" often serves up an outcome we never intended.

Day Five

A MINDSET OF EXPECTATIONS

Just What We Expected

We were slighted.

Shortchanged.

We had an agreement, or at least we thought we did, but somebody breached it. We had an understanding, but somehow another party reneged and took what we thought belonged or was owed to us leaving us feeling wronged and deprived.

Maybe it was as simple as someone zipping into the spot we had decided was our parking space, or a complete stranger failed to hold a door for us, allowing it to swing back in our face. Maybe it was a bit more serious where someone we really counted on didn't deliver on a promise, or maybe a loved one withheld some much needed recognition or attention.

Sometimes it can be almost anything for any reason.

Whether it's money, respect, time, recognition, approval, attention, courtesy, you name it, we are ready to receive and eager to collect, especially if we feel like we're owed because it's very important to get what you're owed. That's the whole point of being owed, right? Otherwise, we'll be left feeling like we're lacking something that is rightfully ours, and it's kind of hard to balance the scales when you feel that way. What can you do? Take from others so they lack, too? Is that how to make life feel fair?

Well, when our expectations go unfulfilled as they frequently do, it certainly seems fair, especially when we can't stop ruminating over how things didn't go the way we wanted or expected them to. At times, it's almost impossible to "let it go", so the last thing we want to hear from someone else is to do just that. As if we have a choice. When other people don't do what they're supposed to or what we expect them to, we can't help but feel the way we do. Someone else took from or, at least, disrespected us. Any so-called "negative" thinking we developed during the process was caused by what they did or didn't do. They are the reason we keep replaying the events in our minds imagining what we could have said or should have done. They are the reason we start many of our days and end many of our nights feeling slighted and owed. If people just did what we expected and gave us what we were owed, the world would be a much better place.

Right?

Well, then why do we have a slightly different standard when it comes to us not always living up to the expectations of others? You might even call it a double-standard wherein we often use one yardstick to measure ourselves and a taller one to measure everyone else, but we almost never seem to be aware of it. Having two sets of measurements, of course, makes it rather easy to point out someone else's dullness while glossing over our own lack of polish. Maybe that's why we're so taken aback when someone else accuses us of slighting them. We wonder how they got so upset over something we barely gave a second thought, why they are overblowing what really took place, and why do they now feel like we owe them something? (Don't get us wrong, it's not that we're opposed to them being owed; we're just opposed to it being us who owes them.)

So perhaps, in terms of expectations, what we're saying can be summed up as follows:

In order for us to feel like an expectation really matters, it needs to be one of ours. Otherwise, we don't give it much thought. Kind of like we don't give our double-standards much thought.

So here's another one to chew on: in many ways, we have an expectation that other people should accept us for who we are just the way we are, but we generally have a slightly different expectation when it comes to us accepting other people for who they are. Oh sure, we may start out liking, wanting to like, or even believing we like their differences, but all too often we end up hoping they'll want to change to be more like us. In other words, we want other people to adapt to what we like while we hang out and be the same.

Let others give more while we give more of the same.

Of course, describing us this way makes it sound almost intentional on our parts, but, generally, our intentions to treat others according to our own expectations are just not as strong as our intentions to get what we feel like we're lacking, and we spend a lot of time feeling like we're lacking one thing or another. We also spend a lot of time convincing ourselves that other people are responsible for those feelings and that they owe us something in order for us to change how we feel.

Have you ever noticed though, that the more time we spend feeling like we're owed, the more we start feeling like we're owed more? As if, in order to feel happy, we *need* more, because what used to make us happy no longer feels adequate. Now it feels like not enough, almost stale and too familiar. It leaves us feeling like we're doing without, so we can't just settle for what we have because now we expect more. Without more, we won't feel happy.

In other words, we've come to associate happiness with "more".

And we've done so because our expectations are preoccupied with "less".

Getting less, having less, and being less.

We keep wanting more because we keep feeling less, and we don't like the idea of less. It gnaws and eats away at us. It convinces us we're unhappy. So, it's no wonder we often feel shortchanged or slighted because we walk around with an underlying feeling that something is being, or going to be, taken away. Without even knowing it, we expect to come up short, and if that's what we expect, regardless of what happens, we often end up feeling like we got less than we were owed. Yet, we never seem to realize that what we got, although somewhat ironic, was just what we expected.

Nor do we realize that other people are walking around with the very same underlying feelings, and the reason we all have these feelings of lacking one thing or another is because we are basing our expectations on things that have already taken place. It's all that ruminating over what happened, didn't happen, or should have happened. We keep reliving the past in our minds to the point that the present is never really the present. It's just another tired, angry replay of us weighing ourselves down with old grudges, disappointments, and memories of unfulfilled expectations. Though, we never seem to figure out that we are the ones shouldering all the added weight. It's like we carry bag after bag of sand to the beach, staring at the ground while we haul one exhaustingly heavy load after another. If we just looked up, we would see that we were surrounded by warm sun, gentle breezes, calming waves, blue skies, and all the sand one could ever need for a picture-perfect day.

We couldn't see it, though, because we were too busy reliving past events of unfulfilled expectations.

So, what can we do?

MAYBE AN EXAMPLE WOULD HELP:

Did you know that race car drivers often train with a strip of tape across their front windshields in order to block their direct lines of sight? So instead of focusing where they are on the track, they are forced to visually scan where they want to be on the track.[1] A similar technique is common for other sports, too. In fact, many competitive athletes are trained to focus their fields of vision far beyond the few feet in front of them in order to anticipate play of game further afield. Essentially, they are training themselves to lift their perspectives; they are also discovering that maintaining this raised, now broader perspective requires considerable training.

In life though, it's hard to raise our perspectives and look ahead if our minds are chasing events and unmet expectations from a few days, years, or even minutes ago. And sometimes it really feels like a chase. As though, if we just keep thinking about it long and hard enough, somehow we'll catch up with the past and miraculously change it. The truth of it is, though, the longer and harder we think about it, the more attached we become to our expectation of what we wanted but perhaps, didn't get from the past. So if we are constantly looking back, we will forever remain attached to that one thing, that one person, that one outcome, or that one solution we expected to make us happy.

We can almost hear ourselves saying: "But if I can just get that one thing, then I'll be happy."

Well, the interesting thing about happiness is that what we think makes us happy today is usually different from what we thought made us happy a year ago. Just as it will be different from what a year from now we will think makes us happy then. The same holds true for ten years from now, as well as ten years ago, and it's all the result

1 Source: Turnfast.com, The Road Racer's Reference Center, http://turnfast.com/tech_driving/driving_visualfield

of expectations we set. Not only do we determine what happiness is to us, but we also set the expectations for our own happiness. Of course, the more narrowly we set the expectations, the more frustrated we get when anything and everything unexpected disrupts the parameters we outlined to expect. And they *are* parameters. They are our parameters. Regardless of whether our expectations are reasonable, unreasonable, or of little consequence, they are the instructions we give ourselves which spell out the limits of what we want and what we don't. Then we attach ourselves to these expectations, and the more attached we become, the more they limit us to expect and accept only what we've instructed.

Maybe that's why we have such a hard time letting go and why we're so affected when our expectations go unfulfilled. We are attached. Sometimes we feel just as attached as if we were harnessed to a tandem skydiver free-falling toward the earth. We are counting on that other person to help us land safely.

Sometimes they will, but sometimes they won't. Even in dire situations, people won't always do what we expect; they may compromise agreements, understandings, or expectations we felt surely could be taken for granted, only to walk away and never give us a second thought.

But honestly, there will be occasions when we will do the same: we will let others down. We will leave things unsaid, including important things that others expected to hear or wanted to know. We may even decide we can no longer fulfill their expectations and then willfully, reluctantly, or perhaps, unknowingly leave them behind feeling slighted and owed.

Good, bad or indifferent, sometimes expectations go unfulfilled, but how we react to that lack of fulfillment, to that all too familiar feeling of "less" will have a far greater impact on our lives. It really will. It always does.

So we have a choice.

Either we can remain attached to expectations which keep us rooted to the past, or we can adjust our expectations by acknowledging that the only thing we can ever change about the past is how we feel about it. And feeling like we can let go of things that already have taken place is the most natural way to bring into focus what is currently taking place or about to.

It's a matter of lifting our own perspectives, which comes from managing expectations, and it does involve some management. So let's be clear: managing expectations does not mean letting everyone off the hook. Nor does it mean releasing everyone from our agreements, but it does mean that when other people don't do what we expect, we focus less on what they owe us, and more on what we owe ourselves. And we owe ourselves extrication from unproductive expectations to which only we remain attached.

We also owe ourselves the realization that we made those expectations, and we did so in order to feel like we were attached to something. See, we use our expectations and, more specifically, our attachments to them to bring meaning, purpose, and predictability to our lives, so much so that, at times, we become dangerously dependent on them. Therefore, we owe it to ourselves to keep that dependency in check.

Finally, we owe ourselves and everyone around us a more equitable standard: one that raises the bar for us as high as we raise it for them. If we do so, we won't feel nearly as slighted when other people miss their clearance, and we won't feel nearly as affected when they don't meet our expectations because we'll recognize that whatever occurred may have had little or nothing to do with us.

But even if it does, we'll be ready.

We'll just lift our chins a few degrees and resume our training to focus above and beyond just what we expected.

Life is less about the facts and more about how we feel about the facts as we see them.

Day Six

A MINDSET OF NEEDING TO BE RIGHT

A Hollow Ambition

What if we each had the ability to step back and watch ourselves in conversations with others? How often would we catch ourselves inserting a need to be right? Have you ever thought about yourself as having such a need? Or is that a characteristic we might be quick to spot in others but not ourselves?

We rarely think about it but, on any given day, we're likely to encounter someone with whom we disagree about something, and most every disagreement will give rise to some level of resistance. Someone will be pushing their ideas one way, and we'll be pushing ours against theirs. Despite all the pushing though, we'll likely maintain our stance, even if we do so silently because something inside of us will want to be right and because, more often than not, the alternative is we will have to be wrong, and no one likes that.

**But everyone likes to be right.
The world is obsessed with it.**

Maybe that's because being right feels so good. It feels just. It feels like we're winning. It brings on a sense of power which has an uncanny way of making us believe that whoever has the power got it from being right. It's how we often assume they came into power. More and more people believed or were converted to believe they were right, so the belief, as well as whoever got the power, became more powerful.

Needless to say, the world is also obsessed with being powerful.

So it should come as no surprise that, in one way or another, we always are seeking power, and we always are seeking to be right.

Have you ever noticed though if you want something to be right, then you likely believe it is? Or, if you want something to be wrong, then you likely believe that, too?

So, a lot of what we believe is right or wrong is simply what we want to believe.

And we want to believe we're right.

So we fill our minds with thoughts, ideas, and opinions that line up with our particular version of "right". Although we may try to compare and contrast other versions, we rarely give them as much time, thought, or energy as we give our own because doing so might mean we'd have to consider changing some of the things we want to believe.

Although we're often aware that we believe something, we're seldom aware that we want to. We're also not aware that our values come from the things we feel right about, and that's partly because we value feeling like we're either right or "in the right". Of course, one thing we kind of take for granted is that being right generally leads to something else being wrong. That holds true for our values, too. When something falls outside of our values, we're quick to conclude that it's just wrong.

For example: try to start a conversation about something that's as divisive as abortion, evolution, whether or not there is a God, or even whether the Super Bowl should give Justin Timberlake a do-over at the next halftime show, and watch how any room splits in half. Even though it's kind of unpleasant to choose examples that are so emotionally charged (especially that last one), they help to make the point, which is: regardless of which side of the room we choose to stand, we want to take sides.

We need to take sides.

Even if we have limited knowledge or familiarity about the issue at hand, as soon as we're presented with two sides, we almost always take the bait and get hooked on the idea there are only two sides, and then we pick one. In very short order, we latch on to a couple points we relate to and then become highly committed to one side and equally opposed to the other. See, once there are two sides, one has to be right, and the other has to be wrong. Naturally, the more emotional we feel about it, the more right we feel about the side we're on. There's no standing in the middle because we often don't think there's room for one once when we're hell-bent on being right.

In other words, there has to be a winner and a loser.

It's practically a sport; that's just how the game is played.

We seldom stop to think though, how our way of looking at things, namely, our current version of "right", will be looked upon as "not so right" in the future. Somehow we overlook that just like we've done to people in the past, people in the future will discount how we look at things. They'll consider our viewpoints antiquated and obsolete. Their versions of right will be mostly about them and where they happened to fall on the timeline of civilization, just like ours will be mostly about us and where we happen to fall. For the brief time that each of us will occupy that furthest point on the timeline, we all will think we have the monopoly on right. We'll think we have the right answers or on track to getting them because we all will be focused on being right. Perhaps if we had the ability to time travel forward or backward, we'd see that everyone's take on right is and always has been a matter of interpretation and timing. In other words, "right" really has a lot to do with right now or right then because eventually, whatever is right will fall out of favor, go out of style, and be replaced or updated by another set of ideas.

It's kind of weird to think about it, but right only exists because wrong does. You can't really have right without wrong. Right isn't really right until it has an opposition to face, but we usually forget that we are the ones who put them that way.

Another interesting thing about right and wrong is that right often becomes stronger as its definition narrows, while wrong becomes weaker as it collects everything that falls outside of an ever-shrinking definition of right. So the more specific we are with our definition of right, the more powerful it becomes and, frankly, when it comes to being right, we like to be specific. Think about it. The more specific we are with whatever we believe is right, the more right we feel about it.

Which brings us to the crux of the matter:

Right is mostly just a feeling—one we look for almost all the time.

If we're honest, we'll see that we are looking for that feeling, too.

At first, it may be difficult to catch ourselves doing so because, just like most everyone around us, we feel like showing people "what's right" is the right thing to do. Sometimes we feel so strongly about it that we feel obligated to spread the word and let everyone know. We may even feel like we're providing a better way of looking at things, and we may well be. In fact, everyone around us may agree. But if we're honest when we're observing ourselves, we'll see that part of our motivation is to position our ideas above others in order to feel that mild rush of superiority that comes with being right. We'll also see ourselves trying to steer the discussion in the direction we want it to go. Maybe we do this because we're hoping to capture a little attention or hurrying to cut to the chase to save time. Maybe we're eager to share an important breakthrough, or we see ourselves as subject matter experts. Maybe we simply want someone else to be wrong, but in all these cases, we're looking for that very special feeling that comes with feeling like we're right.

There's no doubt about it. We love that feeling.

It's why we sometimes jockey for the final word in a conversation; if we have the final say, we can exit the conversation feeling like we were right. It's also why we begin many of our responses with the two contradictory words, "Yes, but". By inserting some contrarianism, we can elevate any conversation that is seemingly headed toward a "right" conclusion, and we, yes we, can make it *more* right. It's how we introduce our rebuttals. It's also how we play devil's advocate.

(If only we could see that the devil has far more advocates than he needs.)

Our affinity with being right or, at least, feeling that way is also why we try to influence and, at times, even indoctrinate younger or less experienced minds to adopt our points of view. Instead of guiding them to understand and appreciate a variety of different viewpoints, we often choose to promote only ours. Oh sure, we may tell ourselves and them, too that our goal is to protect them, but it's often our own self-interests we are more concerned with protecting.

Wanting to feel like we're right is also what causes us to have such a hard time saying we're sorry. Clearly, saying we're sorry means we were wrong. In fact, the words, "I was wrong" often follow the words, "I am sorry". So even if we feel right about saying we're sorry, we still feel bad about being wrong because wrong feels bad. It's a feeling we've come to fear. In fact, many of the conflicts we encounter in life are the result of the fear we associate with being wrong, and it's no wonder we're afraid because all our lives we've been striving to be right while avoiding being wrong.

Maybe some primitive fear of being left to survive on our own if we're wrong is ingrained within our DNA. Or maybe, it's nothing more than our sense of self-importance driving this love affair with being right or, at least, feeling that way. We usually refer to this sense as our ego, and perhaps, because we've been calling it that for so many years, we believe or, at least, want to believe it's responsible for some of the things we do. At times, we even act as if it functions without our consent. Not only do we credit our ego with emboldening our loftiest ambitions, but we also blame it for getting in the way and confusing us. And why wouldn't we once we show how combat-ready it appears when it steps out of the shadows to confront other egos? Then it's pretty apparent it takes only one of them to stir up all the other ones in the room. (That goes for most rooms and most egos.) More often than not, what they're stirred up about is which one is right, but perhaps because they are all so focused on being right, they never notice how much they want it. Nor do they notice how much they have in common with each other: they all agree that only one of them can be right, and any fight to win that title is a worthy one.

But maybe the fight to be right, simply for the sake or fleeting glory of it, is not the most worthy fight. Although at the time it may seem like an irresistible provocation, it so often turns out to be a hollow ambition because the single-minded pursuit of being right not only limits us from understanding and developing other perspectives, it also limits us from seeing ourselves and our motivations.

Now that's not to say that some things aren't worth fighting for, because they are. Competition and disagreement galvanize us to push far beyond our existing limits. And maybe, we simply are using our egos or senses of self-importance to help us push. But if the reason we fight is mostly to be right, we'll never see beyond the limits of our egos. And looking at things through the limits of our egos is like trying to view the galaxy through a pinhole.

It's a very limited point of view.

But it's often all that we see when we're chasing a need to be right. So the next time we find ourselves entering into a disagreement and inserting what feels more like a need to be right, maybe we could step back and watch how it plays out.

Chances are it will play out much differently now that we're watching.

We might even catch ourselves *wanting* to believe whatever it is we believe is right.

We invest so much time and energy in changing how we look, yet we invest so little in changing how we feel about how we look.

Day Seven

A MINDSET OF FITTING IN

What's Really Flawed?

Isn't it interesting that so many of us spent so much of our young lives picking apart our imperfections thinking somehow this might lead us to perfection?

Did it ever work?

Or did all those years of picking ourselves apart mostly leave us with a lot of pieces we didn't like?

We thought of those pieces as our flaws, and the more we picked at them, the more flawed they appeared, and the more flawed we felt, so much so that we often came to think of ourselves as flawed. Once that happened, that's where we focused. In fact, much of the time we were so focused that we didn't notice other people felt flawed, too. Nor did we notice they were just as focused as we.

But in spite of how focused we all were on ourselves and how flawed we felt, we didn't just accept one another's flaws.

Instead, we used the things we had come to think of as flaws to pick each other apart.

And that's just what we did.

Sometimes to the point of merciless cruelty.

In retrospect, it's really no wonder that so many of us spent so much of our young lives feeling not very whole, at least, not within ourselves.

It's also no wonder that we spent so much time trying to be part of one group or another because groups always gave us that feeling of wholeness. Of course, most of the time we had no idea there *was* such a feeling. Nor did we have any idea we were seeking it. We just knew it felt good to be part of a group and accepted. It felt good to belong, like we were part of something special which, if you think about it, is one of the reasons we're so drawn to groups. Groups give us that feeling of oneness and solidarity. They make our flaws seem less noticeable, especially if other group members possess similar flaws. Once flaws are common and shared, they start to look less like flaws and more like similarities, and similarities are precisely what keep groups together. So, dissimilarities become noticeable very quickly and are soon looked upon as flaws.

Looking back, it's clear now that for us to gain entry into whatever group it was, our flaws and dissimilarities had to be hidden or corrected.

And that's just what we did or, at least, tried to do in order to fit in. There was so much pressure to fit in because if we didn't, we'd be misfits, then all our flaws and dissimilarities would come to light and be seen by others. So we worked really hard at being similar. We learned that the more similar we became, the more likely we were to receive the approval we wanted. It would almost guarantee us entry into whatever group we believed we had to be a part of.

Of course, the opposite was true, too in that we were also learning that if we were different, we would be rejected. Once this happens, it's easy to conclude that different is bad and differences are flaws. But if you think about it, they never really were; they were just things we had convinced ourselves were flaws because we'd bought into the idea that whoever rejected us must be justified. Not only did we accept their rejection, but we also accepted what they categorized as flaws. Instead of assuming their categorizations were flawed, we chose to believe that *we* were, which led to us rejecting ourselves. Had we simply rejected the rejection and not allowed it to become so important in our minds, we could have carried on with our lives managing quite comfortably with our so-called differences. But because we were so determined to gain approval and fit in, we began altering or, at least, trying to alter our differences so that we could be more like whoever had rejected us. Then maybe we could be accepted into their group, and maybe by standing alongside them, we would feel more assured in ourselves. Maybe they would make us feel whole.

Unfortunately, at the time, we never stopped to consider that the group to which we so longed to be a part was comprised of a lot of other people who only felt whole as long as they were part of the group, too. See, they didn't feel whole by themselves either.

That's pretty much why the group came together in the first place: they needed the strength of the group in order to feel strong, so they came up with a certain set of criteria that could unite them as a group. Then they began using that criteria as a means to keep others out. See, if they could keep others out, then being "in" would become much more special, which usually led to them appearing more special. Naturally, the more special they appeared, the more special they felt. But, in order for them to continue feeling that way, they had to be successful at keeping others out, so they worked really hard at it. Of course, keeping themselves "in" was a good bit easier than keeping others "out" by mere virtue of the fact that once you were in, you had far easier access to defend why you should remain and why others should not. On the other hand, once you were out, you had no access, so it was virtually impossible to get back in.

As a result, most of us grew up thinking that being in was good and being out was bad. Being in must be good because so many people wanted to be there. Even though not everyone had experienced being out, at least not firsthand, somehow everyone seemed to know that it wasn't good. Maybe part of the reason "in" seemed so good was because "out" seemed so bad. For those of us who were more experienced with out, we often wondered if the ones who were in ever experienced out, would they come to appreciate it in a different way. Would it show them the value in accepting one another's differences, or would it simply fuel their desire to get back in?

At any rate, those of us who were *not* in felt ashamed and flawed because others had rejected us. Even though the rejection had come from them, the shame came mostly from us, and that led to us spending more time feeling rejected and blaming ourselves for the claims others made about us. We blamed ourselves for the lack of acceptance and for being excluded. We blamed ourselves for our differences, and we came to see them as limitations.

Then, our limitations began defining us.

But those of us who were in, well, we thought of ourselves as special and exclusive. We believed that exclusion led to exclusive, so we established a narrow set of rules that made it easy for us but difficult for others to qualify. Of course, the narrower we made it, the more exclusive our group became and the harder it was to gain entry. We even prided ourselves on the limitations we had adopted. It's how we gained our power and took power away from others. Or, at least, that's how it felt. We were so preoccupied with rejecting and marginalizing others that we didn't notice we were marginalizing ourselves, and we were so busy trying to fit into our very limited definitions of desirable that we didn't realize we were creating limitations for us.

And our limitations...began defining us.

Isn't it kind of funny that regardless of whether we believed we were in or out, our limitations began defining us? Whether we were the ones doing the rejecting or the ones feeling the rejection, we all were shaping our limitations and then allowing them to define us. We were all participating in advancing a way of thinking whose sole purpose was to divide us and make us believe we were flawed.

Looking back, it's easy to say, "Well, we were young, and we didn't know any better."

Yes, we were young, and yes, all of that pressure to fit in did get in the way of us understanding we had choices in how we looked at ourselves and each other.

But now that we're grown-ups, and even though we supposedly have a greater capacity for understanding the many choices at our disposal, we still spend so much of our time picking apart our flaws, pointing out each other's flaws, struggling to fit in, and grouping ourselves together in ways that we know will exclude many of our peers.

And in many ways, we still do it with merciless cruelty.

We still use exclusion to make us feel like we're part of something exclusive.

We still dwell on our differences concluding that if someone is different from us or we are different from them, then one of us is flawed.

But we almost never stop to consider that maybe what's really flawed is our way of thinking.

And that way of thinking continually sends us searching for things about each other and ourselves we don't like.

It's no wonder we see flaws almost everywhere we look.

But all that we're really seeing are the very same differences we've been seeing in ourselves and each other all our lives.

We've only been choosing to see them as flaws which, perhaps, should tell us more about our choices than it does about our flaws.

But it also should remind us of one of the most enduring advantages of choice:

We still *have t*hem.

We still have choices in how we see ourselves and each other, so it really doesn't matter that we can't undo the kinds of choices we've already made. It only matters that we can undo how they affect us, and we can start by recognizing that our differences don't make us flawed. If anything, our differences are there to help us see things… differently. Using our enormous capacity to see things differently is the only way to get past our limitations. Every time we come to accept, even embrace a difference we previously rejected, we break through one of our limitations. So in many ways, our differences lead us to our breakthroughs, the same ones we likely would have missed had we succeeded in our quest to eliminate what distinguishes us and sets us apart.

These breakthroughs that push us beyond our limitations are the same ones which allow us to see beyond our differences.

All we have to do is be willing to see things differently.

That's when we'll see that we discarded some really useful pieces with all that picking apart.

That's when we'll see that our flaws don't look like flaws anymore.

And that's when we'll realize that the only thing that was ever flawed was our way of thinking.

"The difference between you and me: You risk and act, while I watch and fear".[2]

Day Eight

A MINDSET OF WORRY AND FEAR

Calling it Something Else

Something bad has happened or is about to, and that something is big or, at least, to us it is. Along with that something, almost from out of nowhere, comes a feeling as if we were just punched in the gut, and we've lost the capacity to take a deep breath. Each subsequent shallow breath reminds us of whatever it is that's causing us such abject fear and threatening to take control of our lives. Each thought now seems very much like the one before it as well as the one after it. We are afraid, so very afraid, and our minds can focus on nothing else. The focus fills us with anxiety and dread as each and every fearful scenario we imagine submerges us deeper and deeper into despair. We are lost inside a state of mind that allows no

2 Mark Sullivan, Beneath a Scarlet Sky: A Novel, (Seattle: Lake Union Publishing, 2017) page 411

escape. It's paralyzing. Fear has taken over, and we obey; the more we obey, the greater the fear, and the more obedient we become. We are trapped inside a self-fulfilling prophecy of fear which repeatedly beckons us to imagine and expect the worst. So we do as our fears command and spend every possible moment worrying about what is to come or, at least, what we believe is to come. Each worrisome thought leads to another until all of our thoughts revolve around the single target of our worry. In spite of all efforts to calm ourselves, the invasive repetition manages each and every time to find its way back into our heads as if, because it is familiar, it belongs in our heads, as if, because it has nowhere else to go, it only knows to go right back into our heads. So we let it in, and we decide it's just too powerful to stop. The fear is just too great to overcome, and the only way to deal with it is to worry about it. So, we do to the point we are consumed with worry and fear. Despite the fact that neither the worry nor the fear has ever once in our lives relieved the pressure or stress we feel, the worry is what we tell ourselves we need in order to deal with the fear. It's how we cope, even though very little coping ever results. If anything, our interpretation of coping usually makes our fears feel more real.

Of course, while it's happening, it's of little consequence how much of what we're feeling is real or even how much of it is rational because, once fear takes over, it's really hard to distinguish what is rational from what is not. It's also hard to prioritize being rational when something that has happened, or is about to, is on the verge of taking control of our lives, especially since we've spent most of our lives believing that if they're our lives, then we should have control.

So when things we fear actually do happen, or are about to, all we know to do is try and control what is happening.

That's where worrying comes in. Worrying somehow makes us believe we are *doing* something about what is happening. It also makes us believe that if we can imagine every possible frightening scenario and think of nothing else, then maybe we'll be more prepared. Then maybe that gripping tension in our guts will go away, and we can finally take a deep breath again and go back to feeling normal. We can go back to worrying about things that are not so scary, things that now seem so much less important, things we probably shouldn't have worried about in the first place, but we mostly did because worrying is how we occupy our lives.

Yet we never really stop to ask ourselves why. Nor do we ask if all this worrying ever makes things better.

Maybe, in some strange way, we think that if we don't worry, things will have no chance of getting better because we haven't given them enough attention. How are things supposed to get better if we don't give them adequate attention? How are we supposed to prepare? Don't we need our worries to keep us prepared?

Then why, if we've spent so much time preparing for bad things, do bad things still happen leaving us feeling unprepared? Does that mean we didn't worry enough? If part of the reason we worry is to help us feel more prepared, why is it that our worries constantly keep telling us we are not? And why, if our worries never seem to relieve the underlying pressure or stress, do we put so much trust in them? Surely, it must be trust we're feeling because worry is where we always retreat when life starts spinning out of control, even though every single time, our retreat takes us right back to our fears, the same fears which, at some point, we bought into and tailored according to our own preferences.

Of course, they never felt like preferences, especially ones we had anything to do with; maybe that's because we only think of our fears as things we prefer to avoid and ignore so we don't have to feel like it's us who summon them whenever they show up. Instead, we can busy ourselves with worrisome thinking that makes us feel like we are doing something about their seemingly unannounced arrivals.

But in reality, we are doing both.

We are making ourselves afraid, and then we are worrying about whatever it is we've made ourselves afraid of.

But we seldom do any of it consciously.

Instead, we entrap ourselves inside an alternate reality of fear and use our very own worries to keep us locked inside that alternate reality. Though while we're afraid, we can't imagine anything feeling *more* real than our fears.

And that's kind of the point. We imagine things we convert into feelings, and once we feel them, especially if we allow them to feel like fear, we no longer feel like we can manage them, so we let them manage us. By not being aware of it though, it never feels like stuff we're doing; but it is, and it all comes from fear.

See, our worries are nothing more than fears about other fears. We've just been calling them different things, so we've come to believe they are different, but they are not. Our worries are simply the fearful scenarios we imagine about the things we fear, and by using them to make us feel like we are being productive, we never notice nor look back to see that the only thing we ever produce with all that fear is more of the same.

In other words, the more time we spend feeling afraid, the more afraid we become.

Which also translates to: the more we worry, the more we worry.

And usually what we're worrying about (i.e., what we're afraid of) is that we don't have control over what is happening. So we constantly try to get it. Although life repeatedly shows us we can never have it, we still live as if we can, and we act as if controlling the things around us will make our fears go away, instead of recognizing that in order to better manage our lives, we have to better manage our fears.

Which really means: our fears need our attention! They need us to look at them and see them for what they are. They also need us to take ownership of them, which includes admitting we not only create but also use them to work against us.

We've been using our very own army of fears against us for a long time. We've also been trying to fight that army with a different set of fears, namely, our worries. But you can't use one set of fears to overcome another and then be surprised that you're still afraid.

All we can ever produce with fear is more fear!

But by taking an active and responsible role in managing our fears, we can produce much less. And the cool part is we'll end up feeling far more productive because we won't have wasted all that energy and adrenaline on feelings of fear we allowed to get out of control.

See, we've allowed ourselves to believe that our fears are enormously complex, and maybe to some extent, they are. How many times have we wondered where they came from? How many times have we decided they came from someone else? You know the drill, "I think this fear comes from that fear which comes from this other fear, so in order for me to understand all these fears, I have to know which one was first, how long I've had it, and who I got it from". The process, alone, can be quite involved, but maybe a simpler solution to unraveling the complexity of our fears is by simply not thinking of them as complex. Despite their origins or how interconnected they may be, our fears are really just a bunch of bad thoughts we keep repeating to ourselves. We've just repeated them so often that we've made them seem complex.

That invasive repetition is what lies at the heart of our fears; it's also what lies at the heart of our beliefs that we are *doing* something about our fears. In reality though, all this time we've spent thinking we were "doing" and "preparing" for something by using worry to occupy our lives, we weren't.

Being afraid is how we've been occupying our lives.

We've been preparing for more fear.

We've made fear so familiar to us we no longer recognize it *is* fear.

But it is.

We've just been calling it something else.

Running makes it hard to see anything other than reasons to keep running.

Day Nine

A MINDSET OF RUNNING AWAY

A Little of What's Best in Us

We all run from things. All of us.

If we run, we can remove ourselves from things, people and situations we don't like.

We can also avoid confrontation and all the uncomfortable things that come with it. Confrontation is never easy because it means we'll be asked to account for things. At minimum, we'll be expected to explain, and that's the last thing any of us want to do when we're running. In fact, knowing that we might have to explain is one of the main reasons we run. It's hard enough explaining things to ourselves, so we often run from that, too.

At the time though, running seems to be the only thing that protects us from explaining and confronting. So we look for the nearest fire escape and flee the scene. We can't leave answers because that would require us to stick around. Although we know we'll undoubtedly leave behind some turbulence, that's just how it goes. Even if we have to pull the rug out from under someone else in order to sweep the whole mess under it, that's just the way it has to be. We have to cut our losses or, at least, what we think are losses.

Things change. People change.

Naturally, these explanations make a whole lot of sense when we are the ones running, not looking back, or throwing in the towel. But thinking back to the times when someone threw us in with the towels, these explanations didn't make much sense. They still don't. Maybe that's because leaving someone behind feels nothing at all like being the one who was left. It's scary and confusing, and despite how hard it is to shake the seemingly unshakeable memories, we often use it as justification for doing the very same thing to others. It's almost as if we decide that if things happen to us, then that's how life must work, and if that's how life works, then it must be okay for us to work that way, too. Before you know it, we have all the justification we need. No confrontations. No explanations. If we have any doubts, we can simply remind ourselves that we're no good with explanations, so everyone else is better off if we don't. We might even be doing them a favor. Eventually, things will work themselves out. People will adapt. So will we. Then we'll be off the hook. The passage of time will make everyone forget.

But does it?

Or do we?

Since we're talking about running, it might help to clarify that sometimes it's not really about running away. Sometimes it's more like running toward, especially when we're running toward something new and different that makes us feel vibrant and alive and allows us to create new versions of ourselves. Frankly, had we shared these new versions with the people we left behind, they wouldn't have understood, and they wouldn't have liked that we were changing. Change wasn't part of our deal with them.

(Come to think of it, change is seldom part of any deal. Sort of makes you wonder why it is that we make so many deals that don't allow for change.)

At any rate, running toward something new allows us to feel new, too. So, the way we previously saw ourselves no longer matters. Now, we can be whoever we want to. The slate is clean. We've found a new audience, and that makes the old one seem like they just weren't able to bring out the best in us. Now that we're around new people who *can*, we can look to them as the reason we ran.

Even though we were the ones running.

It doesn't really matter that we didn't know why.

We just know when we get certain feelings, we have to run because it's the only way to get away from those feelings. So we run from all the things and people that make us feel the way we do. Since they are responsible, we don't have to think about their feelings. That's up to them to figure out.

In other words, we leave it to them to figure out *their* feelings and ours, too.

We also leave it to them to figure out our decisions, even though running makes it seem like decisions are what we left behind.

Clearly, we decided to run and, although we may not have been aware of it, that decision denied whomever we left behind access to the decision-maker by denying them access to us. Since we weren't around though, we weren't able to see how hard it was for them to pick up the pieces we had scattered. That's because we were focused on running, and running makes it hard to see anything other than reasons to keep running.

Or, to keep us from seeing the real reasons we run, and if we stopped running, we might have a chance to see that, yes, we are running from confrontations, but not from the ones we think.

See, we are running from confronting ourselves and our own feelings of cowardice: feelings that seem out of sync with how we see ourselves; feelings we cannot bear to own because owning them would mean we would have to explain, and explaining would mean we would have to accept responsibility. And since we don't want to feel any of those things, we try and outrun them.

But we never do.

It always turns out that no matter how fast or far we run, those feelings run right along with us. Yes, maybe eventually we put them aside and move on to other things, but whenever we go back and revisit those difficult memories in our minds, the same cowardly feelings resurface, often bringing with them more intensity than the original ones.

If only, originally, we hadn't run.

If only, we had cleared the air, then any potential cowardice would have vanished with the air we cleared, likely never to have become a memory. Instead, by running from our own feelings, we created for ourselves a lingering pang of regret that would feel more irreparable as time went on and would lodge itself inside of us for a very long time.

That's what running from our feelings really does. It lodges regret inside of us for a very long time. It also lodges inside of others a confusion they may never unravel, and we know this because of the confusion we've never unraveled about the people who left us behind as they ran from not only from their feelings but ours, too. So it makes no sense for us to do the same and then try to rationalize it with some fatalistic notion that it's just how the world works. Subscribing to that kind of rationale would suggest we believe that every time someone is left behind, someone else will eventually pay the price and suffer the same fate. Needless to say, that would be a very strange way for the world to work, and we know it doesn't work that way, just like we know that our lives are not about how the world works.

Our lives are about how we work with the world, and if we choose to work with it by running from or toward any excuse that makes us feel better about running, we won't end up feeling very satisfied with our work. But if instead, we decide to work through what are very normal feelings, including cowardice or any other fear, we can end up with some real satisfaction in ourselves.

See, this thing we refer to as "what's best in us" is not something that others bring out. It's something we develop within, and it comes from recognizing and then accepting that we are the source of our feelings. No one gives them to us or makes us feel certain ways. We do it. We only tell ourselves our feelings are coming from other people so that we can shift the onus away from us, and usually, that's because we don't want to admit we have certain feelings, especially ones that feel like cowardice. We have this unspoken fear that if we admit to cowardice, then we'll have to be seen as cowards. But we *all* have cowardice, just like we *all* have bravery, and we all only get to our bravery by working through our cowardice, but it's kind of hard to work through anything without first acknowledging that it's there and that we're feeling it!

It's perfectly normal to feel things, and it's perfectly normal to have the urge to run from the things we feel, but it's what we do with those urges that matters most. This is where we can put what's best in us to good use.

It only takes a little awareness to save us from, what could be, years of regret, and it only takes a little of what's best in us to bring that awareness out.

Maybe it's time we confront a little of what's best in us.

In spite of the damage others may have done to us, the more lasting damage comes from what we do to ourselves.

Day Ten

A MINDSET OF BLAME

The Stories We Tell

If we could total how many minutes of our lives we have devoted to blaming others for our setbacks, would the numbers surprise us?

If the numbers were high, would our first reaction be to blame someone else for the results?

Would our private reactions be different?

Would they lead us to wonder if we have spent too much of our lives blaming other people for things we don't like about our lives?

Or would it make us angry at all the people who, up to this point, have interfered with our lives, our livelihoods, and our happiness? You know them: the same people who have left us feeling victimized. And it wasn't just a feeling they left with us; in many ways, we *were* victimized and, in some ways, continue to feel so. Many things that have happened in our lives have been caused by other people who were at fault and who are to blame. They are the reason we feel the way we do, which is why we've been focused on our need for *them* to change. But even though experience has shown us that whoever we blame does *not* change, for some reason, neither do we.

See, when it comes to them and others like them, we often feel angry and somewhat powerless. Somehow the people who have made us feel victimized wield some sort of power over our feelings, especially our feelings about them. We seldom ask ourselves why they have that power or how they got it. Instead, we focus on what they do to us, and why they are to blame. And with that much focus on the "what" and the "why" of whomever is to blame, we've gotten pretty good with using blame to figure things out.

Truthfully, using blame can be very energizing and preoccupying. It can lead to us getting sympathy and attention, especially if we are the ones who've been wronged. And usually, we get a lot of attention when we use blame to get attention. Of course, in order to keep the attention, the blame has to stick, which is fairly easy because blame sticks most anywhere it's stuck. Blame is plausible and most often accepted as credible. As are accusations. We all know that once accusations catch flame, they burn for a really long time what with all the tongues and fingers wagging to fan the flames. We also know that a juicy story which blames someone else for bad things is almost irresistible; the more inflammatory the blame, the more irresistible the story. So when it comes to blame, most of us have learned to tell a good story and a convincing one, too. We've also learned that telling our stories to other people who can relate to feeling wronged ends up feeling pretty validating for us. And it must for them, too, because we all seem to feel a bit more bonded once we hold a third party responsible for our common wrongs. Of course, once we hold someone else responsible, it feels almost natural to expect them to fix whatever is wrong, even if the things which need fixing are part of our lives, and even though our experience has shown us that third parties we hold responsible seldom do what we expect. Nonetheless, we often act as if our work is done once we identify whoever is at fault. As a result, not much happens to improve the status quo, or at least not our status quo.

So, despite blame's ineffectiveness with raising our status quo, it is effective at making us feel better, at least temporarily, assuming the blame is directed away from us. We all learn pretty early in life that if the trajectory of blame is headed toward us, it is best to get out of the way because accepting blame feels nothing like giving blame, so most of us become far more practiced with giving it than we do with receiving or accepting it. Naturally the more practiced we become with giving it, the more skilled we become with deflecting it away from us.

See, that deflection, that shift of blame, is often what we use to feel better because it also shifts the workload for fixing things away from us. In many ways, getting rid of work is something we've taught ourselves to like, even though getting rid of work, especially work on ourselves or our own lives often undermines our motivation to try. Trying requires energy and focus, and it feels a lot like work, so if we're focused on getting rid of work, we can't really focus on trying. In some ways, trying can feel more like a double-edged sword. If we try and then we fail, we may risk shifting some of the blame, along with an expectation to correct the failure, back to us. This would mean a bigger workload or burden is on its way, or at least, that's how it feels because it often feels like blame, or at least accepting blame, leads to responsibility.

And responsibility definitely feels like work. So if we've been using blame to get rid of work, it's possible we've been using it to get rid of responsibility, too.

Although we may not be aware of it, we've been using blame as a tool, and regardless of the frequency or the degree to which we use it, most of us have been using blame as a means to get what we want or out of things we don't want, all our lives.

But we don't all use it responsibly.

Maybe that's because blame has been very productive for us, especially when we've used it against others. Everyone knows that blame is a quick and reliable way to attract and direct attention because wherever blame is making an appearance, attention is right around the corner waiting to make it sizzle. You can bet that if one person is handing out blame, at least ten people are waiting to hear about it or witness it. So even if we don't think of blame as something we consciously use to get attention, we certainly know that by using it, some attention will follow, and it likely will be pretty good for us, regardless of how responsibly or irresponsibly we use it.

But we're still using it.

And using things suggests some inherent responsibility, especially if the things we're using are tools which are as potentially dangerous and deserve as much respect and special handling as does a chain saw or any other power tool. Of course, we've made sure to require warning labels which caution us about the responsible use for these tools, but we've never done so when it comes to the responsible use of blame. So, maybe it's up to us to build in that responsibility because if it's not used carefully, blame can cause a lot of damage. And sometimes, that's exactly why we use it because it feels like the only tool we can use to get back at the people who have caused us damage. Oh, there's no doubt about it: they have caused us damage. They have wronged us. Some people we've encountered in life deserve the blame we've used against them, and that blame and our ability to use it by pointing out their unquestionable wrongs is how we've emboldened ourselves and earned some much-needed relief, even closure.

But it is possible, even likely, that from time to time we wronged them or, at least, some of them in return, especially when we exaggerated and embellished our stories in order to get the attention and retaliation we sought. Admittedly, at times, we used hostile words and deeds against these people, and by doing so, we led third parties, oftentimes complete strangers, to unfairly mistrust and malign them, as well. In our defense, we were angry and hurt, and when you feel that way, and you're standing really close to it, it's hard to see the big picture. It's also hard to see that anger and hurt are what keep us focused on the little picture, the one that only shows us what we believe is happening to us. See, if we believe we're being victimized, it's almost impossible to imagine that we could be victimizing others, especially when those others are the ones victimizing us. But victimizing is often a two-way street, although when you're feeling victimized, it's really hard to think about the traffic going the other way.

It's also hard to resist the urge to go from that place of feeling victimized to that more deliberate place of playing the part of the victim. Naturally, none of us like to think of ourselves as playing any part, but occasionally, to garner more of the soothing feelings that come with attention, we over-emphasize or over-dramatize our plight. The more we play that role, the more familiar it feels, and the less it feels like much play is involved. It just feels like our normal way to deal with things.

But is it really normal, or have we gotten so used to using blame as a way to get through life that we've made it *seem* normal?

Because it sure seems normal to focus our time and energy on whoever it is we need to blame for whatever it is we need to blame them.

But maybe it would feel less normal if we stopped focusing on whoever and whatever it is we need to blame and started focusing on why we *need* it because our need to blame is what's causing us to think the way we do. It's causing us to repeatedly search for someone to be at fault by making us believe that if things aren't going our way, then someone must be at fault. And since blame is predicated in fault, it's not very hard to find fault if we're using blame to find it. Blame always finds its mark, especially after so much repeated use.

It's that repeated use that convinces us we need it and, before we know it, that need takes up residence in our minds where, if it stays long enough, it becomes a state of mind that ends up responding to needs that aren't really needs at all.

Blame is not, nor has it ever been, something we need. It is simply something we use to tell the stories of our lives.

So if we've accumulated far too many minutes using blame to tell our stories, perhaps it's time to start retelling many of the stories we tell.

There are two things required to find our life's work—one is life and the other is work.

Day Eleven

A MINDSET OF RESPONSIBILITY

Passing the Buck

If you do a Google search, you'll find that the origin of the phrase, "pass the buck" dates back to poker playing during the second half of the 19th century in the American western frontier. The buck, commonly made out of deer antlers, referred to the handle of a knife. In order to discourage cheating and make the game fairer, the knife, which was used as a marker to signify the dealer, would be passed along the table from one player to the next. Presumably, if a player didn't feel comfortable being the dealer, he would pass the buck. Ultimately, in whichever player's authority the buck rested, the responsibility was entrusted to deal a fair game.[3]

3 Historical Dictionary of American Slang, v. 1, A-G, edited by Jonathan Lighter (New York: Random House, 1994).

Although the phrase has lost its literal meaning since that time, we still use it to describe someone who doesn't feel comfortable dealing with a particular responsibility, except now, we use it to suggest that whoever is passing the buck is evading responsibility, usually at the expense of someone else.

See, the way we often view it is that accepting responsibility, especially if it's one we don't want, is hard and loaded with expectations, which is why we often put it off or pass it off to others. Then no one can follow a trail of breadcrumbs back to us if things don't go as planned. If we can pass the buck, we can force someone else's hand so we can maneuver around some of the challenges coming our way. Sometimes that means us stepping aside to get out of the way or slipping behind someone else who'll block the way; sometimes it even means placing someone else in front of harm's way. It's a grown-up game of dodgeball; if we're the people who are better at dodging responsibility, we tend to get better at dodging as times goes on; if we're the people who get hit with responsibility, we often don't see it coming.

Simply put, if we're the responsible type, the buck stops with us; if we're not, we often get a pass for having evaded it, a pass that allows us to get back to doing the things we want. And why wouldn't we? If we can get other people to do things we don't want to, isn't that enough of an indication we really didn't need to do those things in the first place? If we can pass the buck to someone else who'll pick up the slack, how do we lose?

Well, maybe there's more to it than that.

Because more often than not, the things we "want to do" are a small subset of things we've done before or are not intimidated by, you know, things we feel comfortable with. On the other hand, the things we "don't want to do" are often a subset of things we may not have done before, find intimidating or less comfortable. In other words, experience, fear, and comfort are often what we consider when it comes to keeping or passing the buck, namely, accepting or not accepting responsibility. Fear and comfort make it clear that it's easier and safer to help clean up messes than it is to take chances that may lead to them. Experience shows us that once we decide not to take responsibility, it's easy to become part of the peanut gallery that criticizes whoever does. All things considered, it's just easier not to accept responsibility or, at least, that's how it seems in the short run.

But things aren't always as they seem because, in the long run, we often learn that the less experience we have with responsibility, the more we *need* others to do the things we didn't want to do, which, in many cases, turn out to be a subset of things we didn't learn *how* to do. Essentially, our earlier decisions to opt out or look the other way when it came to responsibility were the very things that prevented us from becoming self-reliant. They also prevented us from experimenting with new things we may have liked even more. Had we just experimented, we may have uncovered some aptitudes and talents within ourselves we wanted to develop. Without taking chances though, and risking a little failure, we weren't able to experience those possibilities because we had usurped our own potential. By passing the buck of responsibility, we passed up an opportunity for self-reliance.

Can you remember when you first learned to ride a bicycle? For almost every one of us, someone ran alongside and held on to keep us upright and build momentum. While they ran and tried to prep us, we focused on getting ready to take over because we knew they soon would be letting go. We felt that crazy mixture of adrenaline, excitement, and fear, but the instant they let go, and we realized we were doing it all by ourselves, we felt exhilarated and completely self-assured. While it was happening, we each felt something like: "Wow!! I'm doing it; I'm doing it all by myself. I can do this! This is awesome!!"

Within a matter of seconds, it felt completely natural, as if we'd been riding a bicycle all our lives. It was all us. We were making our own breeze. We were telling the world, "Hey, I got this. I can take over from here." And we wanted to take over. We were in charge of how fast we would go and where and when we would stop. It was a milestone, and it marked a new level of independence inside of us. From that point forward, when it came to riding our bikes, never again would we imagine relying on someone else to do it for us.

Although much less celebrated and, at times, almost forgotten inside the memory of that first solo ride was the "someone else" who ran alongside. Most of us couldn't glance back to witness their satisfaction with our success, but in our memories, we can still hear their cheers. We didn't know it at the time, but they were offering us a valuable lesson: they were showing us that life's best teachers inspire us to handle things on our own. They will be there to help us build momentum, but we will be expected to take over, find our own balance, and make our own decisions. We will be expected to risk a little failure in order to take responsibility for ourselves.

Well, if every experience in life could promise us the same high and sense of gratification as did our first solo bike ride, wouldn't we always take chances when it came to experimenting with new responsibilities?

Maybe. But just like we did with that first solo ride, we'd have to decide to take the chance to face our challenges unaccompanied, without any guarantee of knowing what was in store. During that first solo ride, mostly what we knew was that we felt a little scared, but we didn't know it was the unknown that made us feel that way. Would we fall? Would we crash? Would people make fun of us if we fell or crashed? We didn't know. It wasn't until we made the decision to take the risk and go it alone that we were able to experience the gratification firsthand. And a good bit of that gratification came from overcoming our fear of the unknown. Of course, after we logged several miles on our trusty bikes, we also experienced the risk firsthand because, at one point or another, most of us fell, even crashed. But usually, we just got up, hopped back on and rode home. Okay, sometimes we walked home. But even as we walked, sporting our fresh scrapes and bruises, we unknowingly carried with us a budding sense of independence, responsibility, and self-reliance.

And that's the really cool thing about responsibility and self-reliance. Most every time we take a chance or get back up after a fall, we feel a little less afraid of chances and falls, and we no longer think of falls as failures. We don't even notice how quickly we recover. Without even knowing it, we overcome fears, and the funny thing is that once we do, we barely can remember ever having them or what they felt like in the first place. It's almost as if we never were afraid of whatever it was. If someone down the road happens to remind us, it seems like they're misremembering because once fear is behind us, or once we put it behind us, it loses its importance and relevance. We don't necessarily deny our former fear; it's just we no longer can relate to whatever it was as something that is worthy of fear, especially our own.

But by golly, put fear in front of us, or more specifically, let us put it there, and watch what happens. It's a complete game-changer. It's one of the main reasons we pass the buck or look to others to take over, even rescue us. We tell ourselves these other people are more capable, and maybe in some respects, they are, but usually, they are just more willing to risk a little failure because they don't see failure as the end of the process or as an excuse to stop; they just see it as the natural way to figure out how to do things. Instead of using failure as a platform for their own feelings of inadequacy, they use it as an opportunity to rethink or re-do something that needs to get done, which is often how they end up becoming more capable and adept at improving the things they do. In other words, fears are overcome, failures are reclassified, and capabilities are acquired through the simple act of doing vs. the more complex act of overthinking it.

Okay. Fair enough. But why is it so important to be responsible, capable, or even self-reliant if we have all these other people in our lives encouraging us to be dependent? Isn't our dependency on them what gives their lives purpose? Don't they need us to need them?

Perhaps, but then our lives become less about us and more about their need to bring meaning to their lives through our dependency. Although they may think they are protecting us, they often, but unknowingly, are securing their seat at the center of our universe through repeatedly reminding us how vital they are. As a result, our direct exposure to failure is significantly curtailed. By not being allowed to experience and, perhaps, more importantly, recover from failure, we learn that success is only possible if they are present, and failure is guaranteed if they are not. (Which is something far different from what they think they are teaching.) While it's happening though, none of us can see that they are afraid to let us fail and, because they are afraid, they shield us from responsibility causing us to be afraid, too. If only they could remember how others before them had allowed them to fail in order to experience the satisfaction and value that comes from responsibility. If only they could see that responsibility is best shared, not hoarded.

See, one of the most intrinsic elements of being responsible is teaching others how to be that way, too. Without that component, responsibility can easily descend into a demonstration of how essential one person or group is to an operation while the rest of us kind of get lost in the shuffle. We learn to sit passively on the sidelines and not take risks, but what we *don't* learn is that there's also great risk in not taking risks. And that great risk is this: the more we avoid taking risks, the more afraid of risk-taking we become. In other words, the insistence to protect us from failure is what makes us afraid to try.

Simply put, without knowing failure, we won't know how to recover from it. Without falling down, we won't know how to get back up. It's the getting back up that gives us the courage to take responsibility. It's the getting back up that proves to us we can rely on ourselves. Perhaps what we're saying is that a better way to protect us is to stop protecting us from failure. That's how we'll start feeling more responsible within ourselves. It's also how we'll start feeling more responsible toward one another. Which leads to some very nice feelings: like kindness, patience, and acceptance. It's true. When we open ourselves to accepting things we previously shied away from, we open ourselves to greater feelings of acceptance, and that includes each other, too.

Think of it this way: responsibility is just opportunity in disguise. It's not meant to be dodged or avoided; we've just made it seem that way because we've been denying ourselves access to it. We may have thought we were passing the buck, but what we really were passing up were opportunities.

It's easily remedied, though.

It's a matter of taking a seat at the table and joining the game.

That buck will soon come around again and land in front of us, and when it does, we simply need to reach for the deck and let the other players know:

"Hey, we got this."

It's *our* turn. Let's take it and deal.

Why is it we can't recognize our own undoing until we're undone?

Day Twelve

A MINDSET OF CONTROL

Where We Excel

Ask a controlling person if a better long-term objective would be to control more or to worry less.

The obvious answer would be: "Give us more control so that we can worry less."

See, if we're controlling, not having control is mostly what we worry about. As far as we're concerned, control fixes everything, which is why we're always looking for it. It's also why we're always looking for things to fix. If we can take charge and fix things, then we'll feel like we have control. We'll also feel like we're the solution to whatever needs fixing; that gets a little tricky because seeing ourselves as the solution often sets us on a path to searching for a problem. So, at times, we end up trying to fix things that really aren't broken; they're just works in progress being managed by others.

We don't usually see it that way though; we see works in progress as opportunities to demonstrate better ways of doing things which often lead to us interfering, overlooking, even disrupting other solutions already underway. But here again, that's not how we see it because, usually, we're busy pushing our solutions so that others will see things *our* way. As a result, we end up developing a great deal of experience with pushing, often to the point where others see us as being rather pushy. We seldom mean to offend, but our focus on taking charge and feeling in control often prevents us from seeing that we were responsible for their departure. Had we shifted our focus, we might have discovered that our desire to feel in control almost always overshadows the desires of others to feel whatever it is they're wanting to feel.

See, our desire to feel that way almost never allows us to shift our focus away from that feeling; and there's the rub: we don't like allowing. It leaves too much to chance and too little to us. Unless we can decide how things are supposed to be, we won't feel happy. To us, happiness is restricted to a certain set of variables coming together under a certain set of conditions enabling a certain set of outcomes. In other words, our happiness comes from certainty. We know exactly what happiness looks and feels like, so if it looks and feels like anything else, it just can't be happiness. Even though happiness can be a whole lot of different things if people just allow it, allowing doesn't allow us to feel in control. So maybe it kind of makes sense that when things don't go our way, our happiness is often in jeopardy.

Perhaps at some point early in life, we decided that happiness never seemed to be around when things felt out of control because those early, out of control moments brought with them the kind of uncertainty that never seemed to end well for us. So we grew up dreading uncertainty. It made us feel far too nervous on the inside, and since we didn't know how to fix those inside feelings, we decided to fix things on the outside. The more we did, the better we felt. At first, we started with really small things within our young and rather limited sphere of influence. That led to us wanting to fix bigger things and more things; the more things we fixed, the more certainty we felt until eventually, certainty began to feel like happiness. Without even knowing it, we were teaching ourselves that happiness was the absence of nervousness. So, we made a practice of doing things that made us feel less nervous; the more we practiced, the more natural it felt. Which, really, is the purpose of practice: it takes something that, at first, may not feel very natural and converts it to something that does. Once it feels that way, the less aware we may be of how what we we're doing is affecting others, especially if they're interfering with what now comes to us so naturally.

That's why whenever we come across situations which need fixing, we think we're the natural choice for taking charge, so we step in to lead. But oftentimes, we confuse leading with taking charge and taking over. In many ways, we see them as one and the same, and we're not alone. Lots of people are completely happy being led by someone else who takes charge. (Naturally, we get on quite well with these people.)

But what many of us miss is that leadership is so much more than taking charge and taking over. Come to think of it, when you're being led, it doesn't feel like something is being "taken", at all; it feels more like something is being given, like direction, advice, know-how, even support. Maybe, good leaders have figured out that the feelings you leave with others are a truer indication of your effectiveness and ability to lead. Perhaps, leadership is less about what you take away and more about what you leave behind, especially if what you leave behind inspires others to trust in your ability to lead.

So, is trust what lies at the heart of true leadership and distinguishes it from control? Does the ability to inspire trust in others begin with a willingness to trust in ourselves? Perhaps a motivation to control belies that willingness. Maybe a love of certainty is not about certainty, at all, but simply about an unwillingness to trust, even ourselves.

Although if we stepped back and watched, it may look like we are the only ones we trust. See, a long time ago, we gave up trusting other people to do what needed to be done because they dropped the ball so many times. After repeatedly being left to pick it up, we stopped noticing our reluctance to pass it, as well as how long we held on to it. If the ball remained in our possession, we could remove the risk that someone else may not do with it what needed to be done or, at least, what we thought needed to be done. After maintaining possession for a while, you start assuming ownership; you come to feel like whatever it is you're involved in belongs to you. So, things that may start out as a team effort often end up with little effort from the team, and without effort, there's really not much team. That's not to say we won't feel satisfaction from our individual efforts, but without a team, we likely won't be able to share those feelings. Had the other players just done their part, and had we been able to trust them to do so, there might have been more satisfaction all around. Instead, we all sort of fell into a rather clumsy rhythm of how things were to be done and who was to do them. They ended up doing less, often because they knew we would get it done, and we ended up doing more because their way of doing things was less than we hoped for.

See, one of the more challenging aspects of being controlling is being expected to carry a disproportionate share of the workload, but we often end up accepting these heavier burdens because we've taught ourselves the rest of the world never runs as quickly, efficiently or productively as it should. Since we pride ourselves on all three of these things, we feel that our individual contribution is vital to changing the world. Unfortunately, we sometimes lose sight of the idea that bigger change and more widespread feelings of vitality are possible, even sustainable when we inspire others to be part of that change. Instead, if we're trying to control, we forge ahead with a "my way is best" kind of mindset which keeps us focused on what is mine and protecting it as opposed to cultivating a more collaborative mindset with other people who want to protect it, too, because we've made it feel like *theirs*. Without those kinds of feelings, other people end up feeling tired of our way of doing things and uninspired by our way of seeing things. When you're operating from a controlling point of view though, you're not really focused on other people's feelings; as a result, you tend to underestimate how much their feelings impact your ability to get things done. See, other people's feelings were one of those "outside" things we never really learned to control. We were more concerned about the things they did vs. how they felt about those things. Since we were burdened with more responsibility, we didn't have time to think about their feelings; we had too much to do. We also didn't have time to think about our own feelings. Frankly speaking, when things need to get done, you can't make time for feelings that get in the way of getting things done. Right? Isn't a big part of our ability to get things done due to the fact that we don't focus on feelings?

Perhaps.

But is there a cost for such single-mindedness? As much as we may want to believe that feelings are immaterial to outcomes, it might be wise to consider that some of that single-mindedness comes from our much practiced habit of treating our individual worlds like giant to-do lists so we don't have to acknowledge our underlying fears about uncertainty. In other words, if we don't do everything we're supposed to do in the order it's supposed to be done by the timetable we've allotted, our worlds will collapse. And then, what will we do? How will we manage? Well, if you ask our fears and all the feelings driving them, we *won't* manage. We've taught ourselves that without all these things in place, we can't even trust ourselves. And not being able to trust yourself, especially if you're unknowingly depending on a lot of activities to compensate for it, adds a lot more weight to an already overly-burdened state of mind.

That's what happens when we ignore our feelings. Over time, they stop feeling like feelings and more like intrusions.

When you don't pay attention to feelings, especially your own, you can't figure out what they are, and you certainly don't know what to do with them when they show up, so you mostly just want them to go away, which, if you think about it, is exactly what we've been doing all along. By substituting "doing" things in place of "feeling" things, we've tricked ourselves into believing we got rid of those feelings.

But if you take away all the things we do, those feelings come racing back.

See, we've placed our trust in those things. Without those things, there's really very little trust but a lot of out-of-control feelings.

Instead of using control to control our feelings, we've been using it as a way to cope with feelings we couldn't control.

But that's where we're wrong.

Our feelings are the only things we can control.

It just takes practice.

And fortunately, that's where we excel!

Why hold people in the future accountable for things that took place with other people in the past?

Day Thirteen

A MINDSET OF TRUST

Just a Dance

Every relationship we encounter in life involves trust. In professional relationships, we expect the terms of trust to be spelled out fairly clearly, but in personal ones, we often proceed without either party acknowledging or admitting that trust and the terms for it are being established. We don't exchange words to frame what is happening; we just sort of meander our way through a series of twists and curves hoping to figure each other out. It's how we get to know each other. It's like a dance. Although sometimes, it's more like an "avoid-dance".

We draw imaginary lines of demarcation around ourselves which separate us from the rest of the world, and we expect other people to respect these lines. We consider them our boundaries, our personal space; and part of what we are expected to figure out in life is where these lines are drawn for other people. Despite how similarly they may be drawn, no one's lines are the same. The difficult thing, though, is that we often don't discover the lines until we cross one.

In newer or developing relationships, our imaginary lines shift a bit more frequently while we figure out how much trust we are willing to risk in exchange for how much attention we are hoping to receive. But again, it's something we have to feel our way through; we seldom talk about it, at least not with our "dance" partner. It's just not part of the dance, especially when we hope the dance will lead to something more.

So, we tread rather lightly avoiding each other's toes because any misstep could put an end to the music. That's the funny thing about these dances: you can't always hear the music, so it's hard to tell when it stops. The subtlety, though, is mostly by design. The more mysterious we can make the dance, the less obligation each partner feels in terms of signaling their moves, particularly the next one. Without even knowing it, we're teaching ourselves, as well as each other, that secrecy is the best way to define, even fortify, our boundaries. As a result, instead of dancing *with* one another, it feels more like we're dancing around one another, but it's almost to be expected, especially when we move in and out of relationships; it's just part of the dance.

The truth, though, is we are trying to figure out if we can trust each other and whether or not a relationship, or the continuation of one, is worth the risk. We're trying to figure out our terms for trust while gauging our risk of getting hurt.

See, that's what trust really is.
It's our estimation of how likely we are to get hurt.

Of course, we don't often describe it that way. We prefer to think of trust as some sort of understanding or reliability indicator that someone else will do what we think they will or, if we're lucky, say they will. As long as we have trust, our vulnerability to someone else's power over our feelings will be protected. We won't be disappointed, caught off guard, cheated or betrayed.

In other words, we won't be hurt.

And not getting hurt is what makes trust so valuable, but if you think about it, trust is nothing more than a feeling we have that makes us feel protected against hurt. Kinda' makes sense why we don't talk about it: we don't want other people to know that, not only, can we be hurt but, in many ways, we're afraid of it, too.

So, it's not really trust we value; it's not getting hurt we value.

Despite how much we value it though, we almost never speak of it. Even though trust, or the fear we associate with it, is always in the backs of our minds, the fronts of our minds and fundamental to every relationship, the few discussions we have about it are reserved for those times when the terms we assumed could be taken for granted were violated.

Whether or not we're aware of it, we have many people in our lives with whom we never would consider disclosing or discussing the basic terms of trust in our relationships, yet we hold these same people accountable to our unclear, unspoken terms. In other words, we hold other people accountable for our fears we won't disclose to them.

Hmmm.

And usually, these are the same people we think we can trust, even though we behave as if we can't trust them enough to tell them what we're afraid of. Sounds like we've led ourselves to believe that talking about trust puts us at even greater risk of being hurt.

Guess it's no wonder we step on each other's toes and can't anticipate each other's moves when we dance. Our feelings and fears keep getting in the way causing us to step in front of or away from each other. To state it more plainly, without trust, we don't make very good partners.

But it's not for the reasons we may think.

See, we keep thinking that other people are responsible for how we approach trust because, at some point, someone we trusted to not hurt us ended up hurting us anyway. So in order to avoid hurt in the future, we decided to avoid trust. Instead of attributing our hurt to some hurtful episodes and then moving on, we standardized our assumptions about hurt for people in general, including ones we had not yet met. By doing so, we made it hard for ourselves to see that not only would hurtful memories influence our future behavior, but our assumptions about hurt would influence us even more. They would serve as the guideposts for what would become our unspoken terms for relationships, including our terms for being more secretive. Our rationale was: the less we share with other people and the less they know about our vulnerabilities, the less likely we were to get hurt.

In other words, our ideas about trust have been mostly about secrecy and how to avoid getting hurt, instead of them being about the relaxed feelings that are possible when we're not making ourselves afraid. See, the way we've been managing trust, or the way it's been managing us, has caused us to miss out on the many joys of connecting with someone that are only possible when we stop letting our fears get in the way of those connections.

And that, my friend, is a big miss.

It takes us a long time to learn (and even longer not to learn) that most of the decisions we make out of fear usually lead to more fear. So, if the fear of getting hurt is ultimately what we want to avoid, wouldn't it be wise to approach that fear a little differently?

Isn't a big part of why we're afraid a direct result of having spent so much time convincing ourselves that the only way to feel better about hurt is to avoid the possibility of it? Not even the actual hurt, itself, but the possibility of it. That's what avoiding fear mostly involves: a lot of time and energy spent avoiding the possibility of it. Since possibilities, especially imaginary ones, are endless, our fears about them can be, too.

We've been working from the premise that if we overcome our reliance on trust, especially in other people, things will get better; unfortunately though, the removal of that reliance often makes us kind of bitter, more secretive, skeptical, and less willing to trust. If we enter into relationships preoccupied with fear, or the avoidance of it, we almost always exit those relationships consumed by our preoccupations. Granted, other people have hurt us and violated our trust, but after they did whatever they did, they had no bearing over how we decided to manage our fear of those things happening in the future. If we used their betrayals to frame our own assumptions and expectations about how other people in the future would treat us, well, that was totally our call.

The solution is not to eliminate relationships; the solution is to eliminate our fears *about* relationships, especially if a good portion of the time we're spending "in" relationships is, actually, time we're spending in our heads preoccupied with fears about things that might happen in those relationships. Knowingly or unknowingly, if we're focusing on guessing someone else's next move while secretly planning our own, we'll never be able to experience the joy of relating in the moment.

And relating, especially in the moment, is what leads to relationships...and trust.

Otherwise, it's just a dance.

Why keep repeating the same grade in the school of hard knocks?

Day Fourteen

A MINDSET OF COMFORT AND CHANGE

Our Own Footprints

Although we regularly take inventory of many of the "things" in our lives, we seldom take stock of ourselves. Unless something happens externally which shakes us up internally, we move through life somewhat absent-mindedly as we go about our many daily routines. We go to the same places, do the same things, and even think many of the same thoughts as we step again and again in the familiar paths of our own footprints.

And for the most part, we like it.

We call it the "comfort zone".

In the comfort zone, each day is like an intentional replay of the day before, so our lives end up being much like a movie we watch over and over again. We know how it starts, how most scenes will play out, and how each day's movie will end because it ends pretty much the same every day. And we like it because it feels familiar, predictable, and safe. It may not necessarily bring us fulfillment or happiness, but it brings us what we know and can expect and, because it feels familiar, we come to associate it with good.

Familiar is good, so by default, unfamiliar is not as good.

Of course, there are times we realize that familiar doesn't feel very good; we may even realize it's not that good for us, but we still value it because of the familiarity. At least we know what we can expect. At least we know what we can trust, and since we can only trust what we know, we're better off resisting anything we don't.

As a result, we resist change.

Everyone knows the comfort zone is not comfortable with change, so in order to remain that way, change is precisely what we resist. We seldom notice any resistance though, at least, not in ourselves. As long as we're doing what we know and feels comfortable, we think everything is going along just fine, and if things are fine, resistance is not something we imagine ourselves feeling.

For some strange reason though, despite all this comfort and familiarity, we often find ourselves feeling stagnant, unmotivated, frustrated, unhappy, or even trapped. You know: the kind of feelings we associate with resistance, but when we're in our comfort zones, it doesn't make sense that these feelings could be coming from us. They couldn't be the result of something we are doing, choosing, or even, resisting. So any unhappiness or lack of fulfillment we feel *inside* registers as being the result of things and people *outside*, and we start to believe these outside things and people are preventing us from experiencing our inner desires. Day after day we remind ourselves that the only thing standing between us and happiness is them; if it weren't for them, there would be no resistance. If we could get them out of the way or, at least, out of our heads, then we could enjoy our comfort and keep everything just the way we like it. Then happiness could fall from the sky right into our laps while we keep everything the same.

Well, as great as that sounds, it doesn't seem very likely.

What *does* seem likely is that this phenomenon we refer to as our "comfort zone" is actually the emotional underpinning of our discomfort, and it's causing an internal conflict wherein our comfort with the same and the known is battling a deeper longing for a different kind of comfort or a more meaningful kind of life. But since it's causing strange feelings to bubble up inside of us, we don't know what to do other than resist.

Maybe this discomfort is trying to signal that we are changing.

But doing so scares us to death because change means we have to acknowledge that the gap between comfort and happiness is growing, and the only way to bridge that gap is to step outside of what feels comfortable. Once we do so, we're bound to discover that not only are we the ones responsible for what's happening, but it's up to us to do something about it. Needless to say, that leaves us feeling very uncomfortable.

It's so much easier not knowing or, at least, not admitting it's up to us. It's also easier pinning the cause on someone else because pinning it on our own inner mule means we have to deal with something that may lead to change inside of us. But after spending so many years doing and thinking the way we always have, change of any sort seems monumental, almost impossible, especially since we can't even remember how most of it started. Maybe originally someone told us to because someone originally told them to. (So in that regard, it doesn't seem very original.) Give or take a few periodic updates though, it's fair to say we still talk the same way, dress the same way, believe the same things, think the same thoughts, eat the same foods, travel the same routes; honestly, the list goes on and on. Now, we're not saying our hairstyles haven't changed, but many of the choices we continue to make in life haven't changed much at all for quite some time.

And that's because, at some point, we stopped thinking of them as choices.

But they all were.

They still are.

Regardless of where they came from or how they started, at one point or another, we chose them, but instead of seeing them as choices, or even as habits, we convinced ourselves that these things defined who we were, and then we used them to create limits for ourselves. Each time we did, we marked a territory that warned us to stay on one side of the mark and off the other. The longer we stayed on one side, the safer and more familiar it became until eventually, it became "our" side, and we began to think of it as our comfort zone. Of course, by calling it that, we made it feel even more so. Frankly, had we called it our repetition zone, or complacency zone, or even our zone where change is not allowed, it wouldn't have felt nearly as comfortable.

Yet, all of this "comfort" came from what we told ourselves. We just probably never noticed it was the result of us saying the same things over and over again to the point that they became the words we lived by, our mantra, our very own theme song. It didn't really matter what we were saying because we weren't paying much attention. We were too caught up in the repetition of saying what we knew and was familiar. We were clinging to the known through repetition.

And we do this all the time.

For example, when was the last time you discovered that a song you'd been singing for years had different lyrics from the ones you'd always thought you'd heard? Once you learned the actual lyrics by the songwriter, you couldn't help but think, "How did I miss that? That can't be right." You probably even googled it because you needed proof to back up what you'd just learned. How could it be that the version you'd been singing all that time was wrong? It always *felt* right. It may not have made as much sense, but it surely felt comfortable, and it felt that way because you kept repeating it. You never knew you were losing something in translation because you never knew you were translating, but you were translating what you *thought* to be true into what you *believed* to be true, and because you did it so often, you *believed* it.

That's what happens when we repeat the same things over and over to ourselves day after day. We come to believe our own translations and all the limitations that come with them, but just like our favorite songs, we almost never ask if they make sense. We just assume they do because they are familiar, even though we were the ones who made them that way. And this is especially true when it comes to the things we tell ourselves about ourselves! Even if what we say makes absolutely no sense to the people around us, you can bet we'll stubbornly insist that our "translation" is nothing of the sort. As far as we're concerned, we're "telling it like it is" because, when it comes to whatever we're saying, especially to ourselves, we believe it makes perfect sense, and the more we say it, the more sense we believe it makes.

In other words, we use repetition to make sense of ourselves and the world around us, but the result is that the more repetitious we become, the less change we tolerate. That's why our comfort zones tend to get smaller as our lives unfold. We pare down our preferences so much so that, before we know it, we've painted ourselves into the corner of a very small comfort zone, and it's kind of hard to discover deeper longings or more meaningful ways of life from the confines of a narrow corner. Yet instead of translating it as restrictive, we translate it as safety, and because we do it repeatedly, we come to think of it as reality.

That's why some of us feel completely comfortable scaling the sides of cliffs or doing construction work atop the world's tallest skyscrapers. The rest of us may think these people are either daring or nuttier beyond measure, but the people doing them are just repeating thoughts and behaviors that they eventually came to identify as their own.

See, in spite of how complex we've made it all seem, our resistance to change, as well as any desire we may have to overcome that resistance, depends on our willingness to change whatever's happening inside our minds and then repeat it to the point that it feels like what we know. Repetition is what we've been using to get to know most everything and everyone we encounter in life. Yes, we are creatures of habit, but we only became that way because we are teachers of habit, and we've been cluttering our minds with mindless repetition.

It's our love of repetition that keeps us stepping again and again in the paths of our very own footprints.

Yet, all the while we've been telling ourselves it was our love of comfort and our resistance to change.

Time has a way of softening our opinions.

Day Fifteen

A MINDSET OF RULES

There ought to be a Rule for That

If the number one rule we lived by was to shrink the number of rules, would you think we were living in a strange world filled with chaos and lawlessness?

Well, you wouldn't be alone.

We all love rules. Always have. Rules are everywhere, in every aspect of our lives. They teach us morality and how to coexist; they define our responsibilities, outline our boundaries, and of course, guide and govern us.

Oftentimes the older the rule, the more time it has had to embed itself into our lives so that we no longer think of it as a rule. We just accept it as a given. It becomes one of our beliefs. Sometimes we even regard it as an institution.

But every single rule began somewhere.

Probably way back in pre-history, the original rules started out as agreements. Early man must have figured out that it just made sense to join together and divvy up workloads. We had to agree who would gather berries, stalk prey, make tools, find shelter, stand watch, and even who would mate whom. Of course, the agreements must have had expectations. So, did the early agreements become rules because our expectations for things like honor, respect, and trust were violated? Or, is it because of rules that concepts like honor, respect and trust came to be?

Maybe it was all of the above or even, none of the above.

Maybe it was simply about who had the biggest club and strongest arms.

Certainly, in every society, we rely on rules to tell us what to do. We have codes of conduct, as well as consequences for violating the codes. As society grows, so grow the rulebooks, and the more complex the society, the more governance we seem to want for centralized planning, oversight of societal systems, and reliable access to trade and resources. As a result, our rules become more sophisticated. Since there are so many of us, there's just no way we all could agree on everything, so we leave the rule-making to someone else. Sometimes we don't even have to leave it; they just take it, occasionally with force or the threat of it. Other times, we go through rather lengthy processes to decide who will be in charge of rule-making.

See, being in charge of rule-making is a big deal, especially in complex society and, even more so, for whoever is in charge because being in charge brings with it an enviable level of privilege and prestige but also, a great deal of risk and responsibility. If you end up being good at it (rule-making that is), you can get a whole lot of people to buy into the rules. Naturally, the more people that buy in, the greater the chance that more rules will result. As far as rules go, if one rule is good, then more rules are better. That's kind of how rules work. They stack really well. That's how we end up with rules on top of rules.

Once something becomes a rule, it has a pretty long life ahead because overturning it is far more challenging than creating it in the first place. It's one of the things rule-makers like most about rule-making. People in charge know that once we get accustomed to a certain way of doing things, we start to believe it's the right way to do it. So undoing it, or doing it a different way, usually involves a significant overhaul. In most cases, we can't justify rebuilding something from the ground up. It's easier to stick with the status quo and add to the rules that are already in place. Of course, adding to rules works out really well for rule-makers because the process of making rules tends to be very invigorating. Usually, rule-makers are so pleased with their efforts they want to do more of it. They often end up feeling like they're not doing their jobs if they're not continually creating and enforcing new rules. Which brings up another point: even though rule-making and enforcement are separated among different groups, they are closely tied. That's by design. What's the point of making rules if you don't have the ability to make sure they're being followed?

So for the rest of us who are charged with following the rules, we often end up feeling like we don't have much say in the matter.

We see everyone else lining up to march in the same direction, and we know from experience that it's best to find our place in line. Who are we to question the rules? They're rules, right? We know how rules work, especially when they work according to what we like, and we like this whole business of making rules, so much so that we end up creating subsets of rules in our own lives. Although these rules may seem a bit less complex, they are often more significant because they follow us into the privacy of our homes and, more importantly, into the privacy of our own thoughts.

Which brings us to the underlying purpose of rules:

See, the purpose of rules is to change how we think, and for the most part, it succeeds in that purpose because once something becomes a rule, violating it is now looked upon as bad. Even when the rule is brand new, it quickly demonstrates that following it is good; going against it is bad. It may take some time for those who oppose it to give in, but eventually, the power of the rule wins out.

Rules seem to have inertia, too. During the process of making them, a rule in motion tends to stay in motion, but once it's made, not only does it rest, but it tends to remain that way, and we are expected to adapt. Well, at least most of us are expected to. That's a funny thing about rule-making because, in so many cases, rule-makers often create spaces for themselves which sit comfortably above the rules allowing for a "do like I say, not like I do" flexibility of an otherwise inflexible application of rules. Rule-followers are often in the dark about these privileged spaces, but in the minds of rule-makers, the spaces are justified because, from their raised vantage point, the act of creating rules carries with it a significance worthy of greater flexibility for the creative process. According to most rule-makers, flexibility is just not feasible for the masses because you end up with chaos when you give people the freedom to choose and decide for themselves. So in order to avoid chaos and confusion, rules are used to take choices away, and that's pretty much what we've come to expect from them. You might even say that's what we like about them because we know we can depend on rules to be written according to what not to do. It seems almost contrary to our nature to use rules to *give* choices. Apart from a few notable ones in history, it's hard to imagine any set of rules, especially ones with some sort of official intent to be written with language that highlights choices being granted vs. taken away. Maybe that's why we've grown so accustomed to associating rules with restrictions and limitations, as opposed to choices and opportunities.

See, if rules allow too many choices, then people won't do what we want them to, which takes us to the heart of why we love rules so much: rules make people do what we want them to. Think about it. We create rules with others in mind to keep them in line. So when they step outside of what they're supposed to do, we'll have an acceptable way to push them back inside and hopefully, keep them there. The best way we know to do so is to take away their choices. Of course, we don't like it described quite that way. It sounds more palatable to say: "We've established a new set of guidelines" vs. saying, "We've taken away some of your choices". Oh yes, how things sound is pretty important to us. Maybe that's why we use so many different words for rules like policies, procedures, guidelines, codes, regulations, laws, mandates, compliance, decrees, orders, statutes, dictates, edicts, fiats, ordinances, proclamations, even commandments, and that's just to name a few. Regardless of the words chosen though, the result generally means that either choices are being taken away, or we're being told what to choose, which, although mostly overlooked, is a rather conspicuous paradox.

See, once you're told what to choose, the option of choosing no longer exists.

Maybe that's why we think rules and choice don't go together.

Truthfully though, we're just not putting them together. By keeping them at cross-purposes, we stand a better chance of steering the world in a direction that appeals to us. Frankly, most of the time when we think, "There ought to be a rule for that", what we really want is some type of authority that requires other people to cater to our preferences. We want the world or, at least, the part that affects us, to spin in sync with our particular version of how we feel it should. If you don't believe it, the next time any type of rule is passed that changes things to your liking, regardless of how big or small, take note of how you feel, especially inside. If you're truthful, you'll admit it feels pretty satisfying, almost liberating, like a victory, as if a weight has been lifted off your shoulders, and you can get back to living life the way you think it should be lived. You don't think about the weight being transferred to someone else's shoulders; nor do you think about how they have to adapt. You don't even need to consider that something they may have valued was just taken from them because, now, you don't have to. You have a rule to back you. If there's any question, you just fall back on the rule.

You don't even have to explain. You just point to the rule because rules consistently trump choices.

See, rules make us feel like it is okay to be involved in the act of taking. We seldom recognize though, that when we take something of perceived value away from someone else, we bestow value onto ourselves. They lose their seat at the table, while we gain the voice to fully express our choice, which, by the way, no longer needs to be referred to as a "choice"; it's now the rule. Clearly, our choice must have been better because it outranked all the others to the point that it eliminated them. Right? Now that it's the rule, almost no one will remember that our choice used to be just that. Nor will they remember that what we liked left everyone else no other choice than to learn to like it, too.

That's how we sometimes get swayed into thinking that our preferences are superior to the preferences of other people. We use rules to help us feel this way; we also use wealth, power, fame, and privilege to change rules that don't work for us into ones that do. Once rules work in our favor, the less noticeable it becomes that we're using our positions to overrule other people, including giving little consideration to anyone's feelings but our own. By leveraging the power of rules though, we can act as if feelings aren't involved, despite the fact that every single rule begins as a feeling that something needs to change in order to change how people feel. In other words, if we can make people feel good about losing their choices, they won't realize something was just taken from them.

That's the funny thing about choice: we mostly only think about it when a choice *we* value is jeopardized. Then we take it rather personally. Not surprisingly, this is also how we approach freedom which, of course, is about abundant choice. As far as freedom goes, we don't much think about it either, until someone starts interfering with our version of it or our access to it. Frankly, if freedom has always been our way of life, we don't pay it much attention. We just expect it. If it has not always been our way of life though, we hold it in high regard remembering the lack of it quite well. So, unless we have lived without them, choice and freedom often feel like lofty notions that are mostly meaningless and irrelevant unless they affect us personally, or we feel like we could make a difference. For most people, it's kind of hard to feel like we make a difference when it comes to freedom. So, we usually just leave it to someone else.

We approach rules in much the same way. We underestimate the power of our individual voice, so we leave the rule-making to the collective voice or, even, the loudest voice. They can fix whatever needs fixing, and we can get back to life as we know it; we won't have to be bothered. We can simply look to the collective authority to tell us what to do, and we know we can count on rules to serve as that authority because we've been looking to them our entire lives to do just that! We have counted on rules to give us decisiveness, clarity, and direction, and in so many ways, they have delivered. They have given us structure, order, boundaries, lawfulness, expectations, standards, terms, definitions, objectives, and countless other benefits. If they're well-written and effectively communicated, rules enable us to plan ahead, chart a clear roadmap, and move forward.

In fact, we often credit rules as the linchpins of progress. Of course, we also blame them for overlapping with burdensome redundancies, at times, keeping us stuck in place spinning our wheels.

Perhaps rules bring out the best and the worst in us. They do seem to be necessary and inevitable aspects of life, but perhaps when they become a way of life and we develop an over-reliance on them, we limit ourselves in ways we can't or don't yet care to see. Frankly, as long as rules give us more control, we almost never think about how they might limit us. We seldom even recognize that, once a rule is passed, it will force us to look at something one specific way for a very long time because most of them will outlive us. We'll be gone, but our rules will be silencing ideas that are not yet known or have yet to be thought, and that's what ends up happening when we try to dictate one another by how we see things in the present. See, our love of order changes the order of things for both the present and future which makes it progressively important to question our motives and responsibility, especially when we're agreeing to changes for those who come after us who aren't yet here to occupy a seat at the table. Just like early man, if we're making rules, we're making agreements to live a certain way. Are we doing it out of honor, respect and trust? Are we forcing others to live how we want them to, or are we simply not showing up allowing our absence to give everyone else more presence to decide for us?

If we simply fall back on rules to govern our lives, we will inevitably fall back on them to govern our minds. We will stop questioning the whys and why nots of things, and we will start viewing the world and our place in it solely through the shortsightedness of rules, leaving little room to see things any other way.

But there's always room for a different way of looking at things.

We just need to be willing to make room.

And we need to be willing to consider the next time we think, "There ought to be a rule for that", maybe it's time we took another look.

It's really hard to see ahead when we're hiding behind.

Day Sixteen

A MINDSET OF FOLLOWING

The Herd of Popular Opinion

When was the last time you found yourself standing in line somewhere only to discover the line you had chosen had nothing to do with what you were seeking? After the few seconds it took to figure it out, you may have grumbled about the lack of signage, crowded conditions, or whatever it was you thought led to your confusion, but you probably never questioned your own tendency to politely follow what other people were doing.

Because following what other people do is generally what we do first.

We all follow things, like advice, instructions, maps, traffic signals, weather forecasts, recipes, fashion trends, sports, political opinions, and lots of other useful things. We look to other sources to show us what to do or tell us what to think, especially if those sources look or sound like they have good information; and following leads to a lot of good information. It helps us lead more fulfilling lives by finding out who and what inspires us. It helps us figure out many of our preferences; it even helps us pick our friends.

By combining together the many bits and pieces we've taken from all the people we've followed, we create what we believe are the individual versions of ourselves. But isn't it possible, even likely, that a large portion of our individuality is really just an enormous accumulation of the millions of choices we've made throughout our lives about whom and what to follow? We've grown so accustomed to making these choices that it's almost impossible to know when we're following and when we're not because so much of what we think, say, and do is actually our assimilation of what others thought, said, and did. We may refer to it as teaching and learning, but we could just call it leading and following. Imagine if instead of saying, "We're always learning", we said, "We're always following" or "We're always copying".

It wouldn't sit quite as well, would it?

Maybe that's because we don't like to think of ourselves as followers. We see ourselves as free-thinking individuals, even though we spend much of our lives engaging in our interpretation of what we're supposed to do the way we're supposed to do it, and we rarely give it much thought.

For example, if we made our beds this morning, we probably made them the same way we've done our entire lives. The sheets get pulled up, maybe even tucked in, the pillow goes here and the blanket goes there. Every day the same thing. And the way we make our beds is probably close to how much of the global population make their beds. Most of us never think about it; we just do it. We copy what someone else taught us, and since we've done it without them for so long, we no longer associate it with them. So, it doesn't feel like following; it simply feels like the natural rhythm of our lives.

That's how following becomes kind of tricky because we don't realize we are. We don't notice how we're constantly reinforcing to ourselves the same correct way of doing and thinking about most of the things we do and think. Of course, the more we do them, the more correct they feel, especially if we witness other people doing the same. Most of this so-called correctness though was defined by other people we've followed, and it applies to our habits, routines, beliefs, opinions, as well as many of our ideas. Although we generally assume authorship for these aspects of ourselves, we likely copied them from other people, even if we don't remember who they were.

Well, why does any of this matter?

It matters because our vast experience, perhaps even preference for following and copying, is what makes us so susceptible, even vulnerable at times, to being led or misled down seemingly innocuous paths that turn out to be not so innocuous. Oftentimes these paths are ones we would never have gone down had we given it more thought, but since we were following someone else, it's where we ended up. And it's often where we end up when we don't stop to think about what we're doing, why we're doing it, and whether we'd be better served by doing it differently or, perhaps, not at all.

Throughout our entire lives we've been encouraged and, in many ways, rewarded for following what we learned was correct and for copying what other people did. If we didn't, we suffered the consequences of going against the grain, or even worse, against the herd. But the herd only exists because we, along with so many others like us, agree to follow, and much of why we agree is because we receive reinforcement when standing and moving with others. The herd protects us from standing alone, which is never easy, especially if we're standing for or against something. Even when we have no stand to take, it's just easier to stand with others. We won't be singled out or called to account for our own ideas. We probably won't even need our own ideas; we can just follow the ideas of the herd. The longer we follow them, the more the herd's ideas will feel like ours, and the less we'll feel a need to question them, especially if no one standing with us is doing so.

That's how easy it is to become part of a following or, at least, part of a collective mindset. We stop questioning; we just follow along.

Perhaps a real-life example of this is how we've been following the now popularized correctness of our speech. In fact, we are so assured about its correctness that we even refer to it as "correct", which is partly how it became so popular. But it's also partly why we changed our behavior because, once we all heard it was correct and saw other people changing their behavior, we wanted to follow suit. So, we agreed to adopt new words and phrases describing certain groups of people with the intention to be more inclusive and to protect them from previous descriptions now deemed insensitive, disrespectful, or marginalizing. Originally, these changes came with what felt like admirably polite suggestions to help raise awareness, and much awareness has been raised. But as the movement to make these changes has grown in terms of numbers of followers, as well as corrections, the pressure to follow these corrections has also grown, causing it to feel more like policing than politeness, which is what happens when lots of people pressure one another to do, think, or, in this case, speak a specific way. Unfortunately, once we band together and pressure other people to do the same, our next step, or perhaps misstep, is to single out, even ostracize non-followers. So, we've started singling out anyone who speaks with words and phrases that are not on the approved list—a list which, by the way, is constantly growing and never seems to take into account one's intentions behind the words they choose. It's almost as if we've collectively decided that one's intentions no longer matter if the words chosen are deemed incorrect. Despite the old adage we used to follow that said it was the thought that counts, we are now saying that our thoughts only count if we parrot what we're told to think. In other words, we're rewarding each other for not thinking on our own and shaming each other if we do, but even worse, we're using the same non-inclusive marginalizing tactics we are, supposedly, speaking out against. How can we expect others to recognize our intentions when we don't recognize theirs? No wonder people are starting to question not only our tactics but our intentions, too because it's now looking *less* like we're trying to raise awareness and *more* like we're simply trying to replace one herd with another.

And that's what often happens when we try to influence popular opinion by pressuring one another to follow along. We become part of a herd. Whether we're shepherding or huddling within it, the herd makes us feel good about whatever it is we're doing. In many cases, it won't even need to be correct because the herd will make us feel as if it is.

See, that's what popular opinion really is: It's whatever the herd feels is correct. Of course, the bigger the herd, the more popular the opinion, and the more likely we are to follow it. So, it really doesn't matter if something is correct or not; if it's popular, especially with our peers, we're likely to accept it with little to no questioning. We'll use "what's popular" to determine "what's correct", and then, as crazy as it sounds, we'll use what's no longer popular to determine what's no longer correct.

In other words, we'll rely on a collective mindset so that we don't have to rely on our own. No wonder we have such a hard time changing our minds, let alone, our mindsets. No wonder we have such a hard time figuring out our own inner awarenesses. We've been relying on someone else to tell us what they are. By following the herd of popular opinion, we've been depending on a groupthink to do our thinking for us.

But that kind of thinking, driven by the collective, is often more focused on reprimanding our conscience than it is on raising our consciousness, and it does so by shaming us into submission instead of acknowledging our intentions.

Which is why trusting in ourselves as individuals is so necessary. Without that trust, we become followers instead of free-thinkers, but with it, we feel drawn to ideas instead of opinions because we are driven by purpose, not popularity.

Distinguishing ourselves as free-thinkers starts with distinguishing our thoughts from the pressures we feel to think them.

It's how we figure out what we stand for, even if what we stand *for* is standing *against* the rest of the herd.

Peaceful minds bring peaceful times.

Day Seventeen

A MINDSET OF ANGER

Moving Beyond Anger

We sure seem to be encountering a lot of anger these days, and it seems like almost everyone is feeling it. We're either hopping mad or on the verge of getting mad, and the least little thing can trigger it. A lot of the time, we don't really know what we're angry about; we just know we're mad, and if we're provoked or the proverbial spirit moves us, we'll pounce!

It's not just us, though. It's happening all over the world.

You might even say it's become fashionable to be angry. Civility is out, anger is in, especially in what we read, say and write because so much of what we read, say and write is angry, acerbic and specifically designed to instigate, agitate, and divide. It seems to be working, too, because not only do we feel divided, but we feel like anger is what we're supposed to feel.

To one degree or another, we're all participating. Publicly baiting one another is commonplace and rewarding. It makes for stimulating conversation, as well as, a good fight. We all love a good fight. You get more attention when you fight. Of course, you need anger in order to fight, and since we have so much of it, we're almost happy to fight and give people what they want.

And right now, they want to fight.

With all this anger, we're finding ways to package, promote, and monetize it. We want to make money off it, and the easiest way to make money off something is to sell it a certain way, so we've been selling the ways we're expressing our anger with a handful of labels that don't sound so angry, like "organizing", "activism", "demonstrating", "rallying", and many others, too. It wouldn't sell very well if we just referred to ourselves as "angry", and we wouldn't be as effective in attracting others to our causes and movements. Oh, that's right; we have labels for them, too.

See, by sanitizing the labels we use, we don't feel as obligated to explain our anger because the sanitizing gives us enough latitude to be as angry as we want as often as we want for almost any reason we want. We can use the labels to feel constantly offended or to offend others. If we can legitimize our anger, we don't have to take responsibility for moving beyond it. We don't have to find solutions or work toward peaceful relations. We don't have to think about compromise; we just have to find other people to be angry with, and that's pretty easy these days after having taught one another, including our children, to use anger to deal with most everything. In large measure, it's how we've been organizing and demonstrating our activism. We've been stirring our own little pots of moral outrage by constantly adding more rage to the mix.

We've been trying to effect change by using anger as our sole agent of change.

And it's been working.

Or, at least, we think it has.

We keep telling ourselves we're inspiring change, but mostly what we're inspiring is more anger. Despite our clever use of labels, what we're really organizing and activating is more anger inside of us. And it's a bit of a shame, too, because, despite our often virtuous intentions to right wrongs, correct injustices, and raise awareness, we often end up watching many noble causes fade away into lost causes because much of what we inadvertently raised were tempers, voices, and a lot of opposition to our anger. That's what anger does: it alienates and makes enemies out of otherwise reasonable people. When we're angry though, we don't want to think of anyone, aside from us and people who think like us, as reasonable. So instead, we come up with a lot of angry labels to describe whoever opposes or challenges us, while ignoring that our labels are often just as characteristically appropriate for us. By surrounding ourselves with angry rhetoric though, the kind that makes us believe we're effecting change, we can ignore that much of the change taking place is actually happening inside of us. We're becoming very angry people.

Oh sure, we like to think that a lot gets accomplished with anger, and perhaps, at times, it does. It definitely makes other people stop and take notice, but getting noticed is not much of an accomplishment if it comes at the detriment of other people, or groups of people, who we single out as enemies in the process. Creating enemies seldom accomplishes anything. It just drives people with differing ideas further and further away from each other making it harder and harder for everyone to accomplish the things we originally set out to achieve. It also makes it harder to remember what those original things were, once we become enamored with the idea of winning.

Or, at least, not losing.

We hate losing. We're also afraid of losing, and right now, we are so worked up about the possibility of losing that we're turning our anger into hatred faster than we ever have. We are using whatever means necessary to justify all kinds of hatred, including even nonsensical ones where we're teaching kids to use hate to fight against hate. Are we just not willing to see that hiding behind angry initiatives exploits not only *their* susceptibilities to anger but *ours*, too? Wouldn't it be more constructive to focus on our susceptibilities first?

Sometimes anger becomes so much a part of the way we think that we really don't know it *is* anger. It's just the way we think. So by spending time with other people who think like us, we don't really notice that anger is what we have in common. As long as it isn't directed at us, anger feels normal. If there are enough of us, it even seems cool to feel angry, especially if other people are pushing us to feel that way. But the dangerous thing about anger is that the more time we spend feeling angry, the more things we find to feel angry about. Not only do we develop an ease with anger, we develop an ease with staying that way, as well as an ease with rationalizing just about anything we do when we're angry. Anger is like weeds though; if we don't stay on top of it, it will overtake us in very short order, and that's kind of where we are at the moment. We've been overtaken by anger.

Despite our many excuses for it, how divided we may feel, and how opposed our efforts may seem, we all are moving in the same direction. We are moving toward anger.

We have created an anger movement.

We just don't see it. Nor do we see that our anger probably goes back way before we started using other labels to describe ourselves and way before we joined with other people to express our anger. So, any causes or groups we may have joined have likely served us as well or better than we served them because they gave us an outlet to unleash the anger we've been holding on to for so long. You might even say we're exploiting *them*. By standing behind angry agendas, we haven't had to face how regularly we've been using anger to deal with life.

See, we've made anger a habit, and we've allowed it to bleed over into every aspect of our lives. We're just not aware of it; nor do we want to be because, despite all the time we spend *being* angry, we don't like admitting we are. An admission of anger implies we lost. It means we let someone or something get the better of us.

Or, at least, that's what we've taught ourselves.

No wonder we have such a hard time dealing with our own anger. First, we have to feel like we've lost, and then we have to pretend like we don't feel that way. Meanwhile, we just keep using anger to get through things, yet we never seem to notice how much angrier we get when we do; nor do we notice how little we get done.

See, our habit of using anger to get through things is what's preventing us from getting through things, especially when we use anger to attack each other while hiding behind not only powerful words, but powerfully misleading words that prevent us from seeing what we're actually doing. If we continue to use anger as our agent of change, we'll never experience the kind of change we're hoping for in either, the world around us or the one within us. Angry mindsets and angry movements can only lead to angry outcomes. So, if we mean what we say about effecting change, why not start movements inside ourselves that stand for more enduring change like kindness, mutual respect, compromise, and common ground? Imagine how powerful that could be. Imagine how powerful *we* could be. We could finally move beyond our differences because we will have moved beyond our anger.

Sometimes it is our unfamiliarity with convention that leads to our most unconventional and life-changing insights.

Day Eighteen

A MINDSET OF LOSS AND ACCEPTANCE

Hidden Inside Our Losses

Whether you're saying them, or they're being said to you, the few words, "I'm sorry for your loss" signify that something big in someone's life has come to an end.

Whatever it was, is to be no longer.

Whatever it was is now part of the past and, when we're reminded of it in the future, that part of the past will bring with it the memory of loss.

Because loss is distinctly memorable.

Whether it's from the death of a loved one, the ending of a relationship, the unexpected loss of our health, home or purpose in life, or even from something that goes unrecognized by others, like the loss of our independence or ability to take care of ourselves, we will feel the absence of it for a very long time.

Of course, we all know that loss will eventually make its way to us, but frankly, it sucks when it's our turn because of the sorrow and suffering that comes with it. If the loss is significant enough, we question the meaning of life and the cruelty of pain. We mourn what was, as well as what might have been, as we struggle to answer the unanswerable: why now, why us, why me?

We discover that heavy-hearted is far more than a metaphor. Simple things that used to placate us or bring us joy now leave us feeling knotted inside. The clocks running our lives have slowed to a crawl. How can the rest of the world keep moving while we stand immobile? How can other people be so happy? How are they able to sleep? Why can't we sleep? For the few minutes we do, why do we wake up each time jolted right back into our loss? It's almost as if it overtook our shadow because everywhere we go, there it is. Time is now our enemy, yet the passage of it demands we move on, even though the pieces of our lives fit so differently. Unknowingly, we divide our memories into a before and after of whatever took place. Begrudgingly we begin to construct a new chapter of normal. Despite knowing our turn will come again, we hope against hope that, somehow, we can avoid it.

Because loss, in whatever form, is best avoided.

Or so we've come to believe. Pretty much everything we've ever learned about loss is to do our best to avoid it. So we try to skirt it, even outsmart it, often believing we've succeeded, but one way or another, it shows up anyway. As long as it's not at our doorstep, we're able to speak about it matter-of-factly, often referring to it as "inevitable", but we seldom act like we understand, much less accept, inevitable. How did we miss out on coming to understand the "inevitable"? Why do our preparations for the inevitabilities of loss mostly focus on the possibilities of it, instead of its eventualities? And why in polite society, and many of our households, are discussions about life's inevitabilities, including the really big one, considered indelicate and off-limits, making us afraid to talk or even think about them?

Instead, we spend our lives preparing for the risks of loss while secretly hoping we can avoid the inevitable. As long as we can speak about it in the abstract, we're safe. It means it's not our turn, so we won't have to accept it as part of life. It just happens to be the part of life we never learned about because we always approached "acceptance" as the work that is needed after something takes place, not before.

Is it possible though that waiting until after something takes place, especially something we've tried to avoid, taught us that acceptance is to be avoided, too? Have we inadvertently conditioned ourselves that acceptance is the painful process that follows painful events and is, therefore, reserved for pain?

No wonder we avoid it.

Who wants more pain?

And why are some people so much better at managing it, especially the inevitable pain of loss? Is it less painful for them? Are some people just better at loss? Does that explain why really young kids who are seriously ill cope so gracefully with their circumstances? Is it because they haven't spent so many years trying to avoid it? Or have they figured out some great secret that loss isn't loss at all; it's really just change?

Well, loss really *is* just change.

It's just change we don't like, and part of the reason we don't like it is that it means we have to change, too. It means the road we've been traveling has reached its end, and there's a turning point in front of us. Since we couldn't see up ahead, we didn't know the end was just beyond what we could see. Now, we have to change direction and choose a new path. But we don't want to. So we fight and resist, and then we suffer. It almost seems like the more we fight, the more we suffer and the more committed we become to resisting whatever it is that's bringing about change. So, the last thing we want to think about is acceptance because that would mean we can no longer resist whatever's changing. Acceptance will mean that all the fighting we did to avoid change still landed us in the same place. We lost the fight.

Acceptance means we've been defeated.

At least, that's how we've come to see it. No wonder we postpone acceptance until after a change we don't like has taken place because accepting it means we'll be expected to not only endure our defeat but to accept it and move on.

Doesn't sound like much upside, huh?

Well, not if we continue to view the acceptance of change with as much dread as we view change itself, and not if we continue to interpret many of life's inevitable changes as losses we can avoid.

Because, in spite of how frightening and intimidating the idea of loss feels to us, the actual experience of loss often brings with it some very insightful gains, but we don't usually get to experience those gains until we're on the other side of loss. See, that other side, that back side of loss, shows us that change in whatever form it takes truly is inevitable. Provided we allow it, it also shows us that it's unwise to spend so much of our lives trying to avoid it. In fact, it's often our thinking that we can avoid it that makes our losses so painful. Maybe if we spent less of our lives avoiding change and more of our lives accommodating, even initiating it, our losses wouldn't feel quite as painful or life-changing. Perhaps change for the sake of change is not such a crazy idea because it would regularly remind us how every life cycle is continually cycling through change, and that includes ours. Sometimes those cycles feel like losses, and sometimes they feel like interruptions, but they are all changes cycling through our lives. We've just been refusing to see them as change because change is what we thought we were avoiding.

But change was happening anyway.

The only thing that wasn't changing was our refusal to acknowledge it, which, if you think about it, is something we can change.

See, change makes its biggest impact inside of us; some would argue it's where it makes its only impact.

It's kind of strange, but change doesn't feel quite so important when you're looking back at it. It doesn't feel much like change, at all. It just feels like life.

Because it is life.
Life is change.

And since we know that when we look back at change it doesn't feel quite so important, then maybe we could look toward it with a little less resistance and a little more conscious acceptance.

Otherwise, if we continue to interpret loss as change that must be avoided, we will continually and inevitably find ourselves stuck in our losses, as well as our resistance.

But if we come to see change as normal, routine, even necessary, we'll start to uncover some of the extraordinary gains which are imbedded in change.

They've just been hidden inside our losses.

*If you are struggling to cope with any loss in your life, many qualified mental health practitioners are able and eager to offer compassionate care and effective therapies for loss-related issues. Reach out. Ask for help.

An absence of words often makes for fonder memories than the presence of words carelessly chosen.

Day Nineteen

A MINDSET OF CIVILITY

It May Become Your Legacy

Have you ever imagined how many things you have said in your lifetime which, afterward, someone else carried with them throughout their lifetime? Or have you ever wondered how many times other people have repeated your words, the way you put them together with the message they carried, and then converted them into their very own legacy, of you?

What about some of the things you said when you were younger, or even things you said as a child to other children? Do you ever wonder how many of those children, now grown up, still remember your words? Or, how many of your words led to residual effects which made their way to third parties you never even met?

What about things other people said to you, things that really affected you that you still carry with you months, possibly even years later? No matter how long it's been, you know exactly where to find those memories. You simply return to wherever you left them, and you once again discover that, despite all the work you may have done to move beyond them, they remain inside of you, almost in spite of you, in many cases allowing you to remember the words exactly as they were said to you so long ago.

Can you still picture the people who said those words, and do their words still leave you with the same feeling? If you could speak to them now and explain the effect their words had on your life, what would you say? Would you be truthful? Would the long-held memories come pouring out of you, or would you whitewash your recollection to avoid any awkwardness? Once the encounter came to an end, would you walk away continuing to reflect on the memories themselves, or would you realize they had only become memories because of the significance you had given them?

Memories are just things we have given significance.

And we give a lot of significance to the things people say to us, often without them even knowing. But so do they; they give significance to the things we say, often without us knowing.

Despite all the "not knowing" coupled with some occasional "not caring", we go through our lives leaving behind the memories of our words, while seldom considering how frequently they will resurface or how long they will live on in the minds of those to whom we've left them. While giving it very little thought, especially while it's happening, we are creating legacies for ourselves and each other.

And we call it, "communication".

Of course, we've been communicating for a very long time, but now, the way we're communicating is undergoing a seismic shift. Our words are being displayed and relayed in ways they never have before, and in ways which are causing us to race to get them "out there". We want as many people as possible, as quickly as possible, to hear our words or, at least, see them and read them. In fact, we want it so much that we are actually fighting to get our words heard, seen, and read over any and everyone else's because if we don't, we won't be able to compete with all the other words and messages coming our way.

So many words! So many messages!
Coming at us from so many directions.
We are being bombarded, practically assaulted, by words.

Many of which are being used for no other reason than to get noticed, yet we don't seem to be noticing that by using them repeatedly in such big ways, our repetition and overuse is devaluing their importance, which, of course, is causing us to search for even bigger words with even bigger messages in the hope that somehow, they will distinguish us and get us noticed. Now, more than ever before, if our messages are big enough, we, yes we, can be famous!!

And if we can be famous and receive lots of attention, then we can believe that whatever we did, whatever we said, and however we said it, must have been worthwhile. In other words, if the things we say get us noticed, regardless of their effect on other people, there's a good chance we'll feel justified in having said them because fame and attention have an amazing way of making it seem as if the ends always justify the means.

And right now, with the urges we feel inside and the devices we have at our disposal, we mean to get noticed.

So, if that means we end up saying a great many things that we don't really "mean", oh well. If everyone else is saying things they don't really mean or haven't given much thought, then it must be okay. Who cares if your words get away from you? There's just no time to think about how your words may affect other people. Everyone knows that if someone says something you don't like, you just get other people to shame them into taking it back. That's how the system works. You get noticed, possibly shamed, and then you do something else to get noticed again. It's how we communicate now. It all happens really fast, and everybody likes it. It shows we're willing to take risks. It shows we're part of the game.

Really?

Or is that only true until the game or the fame takes a personal toll on us? Like when we get noticed in ways we don't like with words which feel unkind or unjust, the kinds of words we convert, almost as soon as we hear or see them, into memories inside of ourselves? Do our words now need to be "memorable" in order for us to realize how much they matter? Do they need to affect us personally in order for us to see that our collective carelessness in choosing them may be taking a toll on everyone? A toll that is leaving us scratching our heads and wondering: "How did we buy into this new mindset that is causing us to act as if our words are no longer the basis of civility?"

Have we forgotten what civility sounds like and what it feels like? Have we forgotten that in order to feel civilized, we must speak with civility? More importantly, though, have we forgotten that in order to speak with civility, we must first think with civility which means: we must think before we speak?

Especially now that we're digitally memorializing everything we say!

This race we've joined with everyone else to get "out there" and become part of the conversation is affecting our civility in ways that are unbecoming of us and not representative of who we really are, or of how we want to be remembered.

But we can be a part of this race and even get ahead of it if we just decide to get in front of our civility.

Civility is a mindset; one that is expressed through our words. Words for which we truly are responsible. Naturally, we can't be completely responsible for the effect our words have on other people, but we can be responsible for how and to whom we deliver them, whether we're delivering them to ten people or ten thousand.

With every word we choose, we could be creating memories that have significance. Even if they have no significance to us, they could be living on inside of someone else for the rest of their lives.

But by simply taking a few extra seconds to think before we speak, before we post, or before we press send, we can stage lifetimes of better memories for ourselves and each other.

**Our words really do matter.
They are the basis of our civility.**

So, please, choose your next one carefully.

It may become your legacy.

Although the passage of time allows for wisdom, it does not guarantee it.

Day Twenty

MINDSETS OF YOUNG AND OLD

Changes in How We Look

Do you remember being young and completely unable to fathom being old?

It felt so far off in the future that we could barely imagine it as an eventuality. It seemed almost surreal to picture our faces with the lines and creases which someday would reflect the many years we had lived and the struggles we had faced. We never gave a second thought to the prospect of losing our hair in places we always expected it to be or finding hairs in places we never expected to see. We never noticed how remarkable it was to work all day and play all night or to simply play all day and night. We couldn't imagine any wear and tear because nothing was worn and torn. We had staying power, and we didn't know how to relate to a lack of resilience because we had so much of it.

It's just who we were.

We were young and immortal.

And it felt like we would be young forever.

We saw ourselves as fresh, new, current, exciting, vibrant, with-it, now, happening, cutting-edge, forward-thinking. We were relevant. We were it. We were the future.

Somehow, we didn't notice that we were stepping into footprints that someone else had just stepped out of. We didn't see it as a changing of the guard. Instead, we saw ourselves as different, unlike anyone before us. We were making our mark, so we needed to devote most of our time to thinking about ourselves. And we did just that.

Life was good. We were good.

We had no need to look back because we were having way too much fun looking forward.

So we lived our lives. Of course, there was no time to think about getting old because that was reserved for old people. We were too busy to think about it because it didn't concern us.

Then one day, without warning, we had this feeling inside that someone new was coming up behind us. Somehow we were being transferred from what was considered new to what was considered old. *Our* relevance was being called into question. The guard was changing, but this time, we were the old guard. We were the ones being pushed aside and characterized as slow, out of touch, jaded, and old-fashioned.

As we attempted to deny these new and unfamiliar characterizations, we saw that our mirrors were reflecting back to us the images that, long ago, we had been unable to imagine. Our hairlines had receded. Our waistlines had expanded. Our eyesight had dulled. Our faces had furrowed. We had aged.

And we felt humbled as we paused to think about it.

We wondered: why do we feel less relevant once our bodies show more visible signs of aging? Why do we see young as being better than old? Why do we step up in life with so much hubris and step down with so much humility?

Must we experience firsthand the feeling of being replaced in order to realize that we had done the same to those who had come before us? How can it be that every generation replaces the prior one without appreciating what it took to get there? And why do we believe that when it's our turn, we think we know better?

Maybe because we don't know any better.

Maybe we choose to accept and pass along ideas which teach us that, as we transition from one phase of life to the next, our value diminishes, and the decline of value doesn't really strike us as noteworthy or important until we become part of the populous whose value is declining.

It makes no sense to us inside though because we are still who we used to be, but now, we are so much more. We have done so much more. We have experienced, accomplished, achieved, struggled, suffered, sacrificed, coped, resisted, accepted and listened. We have shared, followed, led, taught, and learned.

- » We have matured.
- » We have lived.
- » And what we may have lost in our outward appearance, we handily compensated with what we had gained inwardly.
- » We had gained insight.
- » We had gained wisdom.
- » We had gained humility.
- » And these gains were no small feats. In fact, they had played a huge part in why we looked so different!

But perhaps, because these gains were not as outwardly visible to others, much of what they observed about us was what we had lost. See, they associated the loss of our youth or, more specifically, changes in how we looked, with a loss of value, and mostly they did so because we had taught them to do so through our example. We had shown them how little we had valued those who had come before us. We had set an example that when you're young, you tend to dismiss and overlook those who come before you. We had shown them that when you're young, you think you have all the answers, and they believed us because we were so convincing, so full of ourselves, and so determined and eager to take on the world. They paid very close attention because they were preparing themselves in much the same way as had we. But perhaps because they were so young, it never occurred to us that one day they would replace us or that we would ever find ourselves at their mercy.

See, when you're young, it feels like you'll be young forever.

But when you're not so young, you begin to see that it doesn't make much sense to give less value for having lived more. You come to understand that as we advance through different phases of life, we truly are advancing, and you sort of regret not having figured it out before. It humbles you to realize that we, too, had disregarded and ignored older segments of the population, and we mostly did so simply because they were older, and because we decided they couldn't relate to us. Somehow we missed the connection that they were just exiting the phase of life that we were just entering, so perhaps better than anyone else, they would have had the ability to understand us. At the time though, that logic didn't seem very logical to us. See, we interpreted their involvement as stifling our desire to find our own way. So we responded by stifling their desire to pass along their experiences and to point out the risks up ahead. Little did we know they were trying to show us that things never look the same when you are looking back as when you are looking forward.

Little did we know that insight comes mostly from hindsight.

We carried on though that since we believed we were different, somehow the issues we faced were also different, and we thought what made us different were our views, our music, our intellect, our technology, our politics, even the world we lived in. In the midst of all of our perceived newness and uniqueness, we didn't see that every fundamental issue we faced had been, to some degree, by every generation in the history of mankind.

So is that why history tends to repeat itself because every generation takes their place on the world stage as if they are the first ones to do so?

Every generation attempts to change the world. We all try to engineer better tools and find a faster way to get from here to there. We all try to figure out how to live longer. We all question the meaning of life and whether life exists beyond our own. And we all cling to what we believe is the genius of our unique contributions, often overlooking that our genius was made possible by an evolution of thought that lit the way for us.

Perhaps every generation's true genius is the groundwork we lay for future genius.

Though while we are center stage distinguishing ourselves and exploring our own genius, it seems inconsequential to reflect on any prior genius we had built upon or any future genius that might evolve from our own. Despite its seeming lack of consequence though, our collective genius from all generations is inextricably linked. Who and what came before us made our creations possible, just as we are making possible the creations that come after us. That evolution of thought is how each of us got here, so whatever it is we think we know better is simply the next step in that evolutionary chain. Yes, each next step has considerable value and in one way or another advances our progression, but it does not supersede the value of the previous steps. If anything, our failure to value those previous steps is what leads us to repeat so many.

So if we aim to distinguish ourselves and advance our generation, it would seem that we would also aim to avoid repeating history, and the best way not to repeat it is to know what the history was, especially if we have the luxury of viewing at least a part of it through the eyes of those who not only lived through it but who lived long enough to look back and learn from it. Presently, most of us have that luxury and likely will live long enough to pass along our own contribution to it. Our hindsight is that contribution, and if we do it well and with humility, we can lay the groundwork for the next generation's foresight. As can they, and so on, so that maybe some of our more difficult lessons in history won't be repeated nearly as much.

One of those more difficult lessons is to understand that it really doesn't make much sense to give less value for having lived more because, by doing so, we are discounting the value of our history, our life experience, and all those valuable lessons that shepherd us through our struggles, our suffering, as well as our triumphs.

Those life experiences are what enable us to advance.

And yes, the more we advance, the more our eyesight will dull, the more our hairlines will recede, the more our faces will furrow, and the more we will experience changes in how we look.

But our greatest advances and the ones most worthy of being passed along will come from the changes in how we look... at life.

Sometimes life's roadmap is full of very narrow roads.

Day Twenty-One

UNRAVELING WHAT WE TELL OURSELVES

Switching Tracks

All of our lives we've been told what to think.

We've also been told how and when to think, as well as what not to think, and just about everyone has taken part in telling us.

Usually, our parents are first; then, it's our siblings, friends, coaches, and teachers. Eventually, it's our employers, medical practitioners, community leaders, politicians, entertainers, news feeds, even the people we stand behind in the grocery line.

In one way or another, more people than we could ever remember have told us or, at least tried to tell us, what to think. And with all that telling over all that time, it kind of makes sense we've ended up thinking much like we were told.

In spite of all that telling though, and even in spite of whoever may have told us, what mattered most was what we told ourselves because we took what was said, thought about it, and then gave it meaning. None of it had meaning until we chose thoughts that made it mean something to us. Of course, it meant something to whoever told us, but it only came to mean something to us through thoughts we chose.

See, we have chosen every one of our thoughts, even though a great many of them never felt like choices, at least, not ones we were aware of. But each one of them, no matter how small or insignificant, was a choice, and we made it.

Perhaps in some cases had we been aware or, at least, more aware we were making choices, we might have chosen a little differently but, in many cases, we still might make the same choices today because the idea of having to be aware of each and every one of our thoughts sounds like the kind of work and responsibility we neither want nor need. We'd constantly have to be reminding ourselves, "That thought came from me", or, "I got a little carried away with what I was thinking", or, "How did I go down that rabbit hole?", or even, "Wow, I just created an entire conversation in my head, and none of it was real".

It's almost as if we'd need some sort of governor inside our minds to regulate our own supply of thoughts while simultaneously keeping watch over the governor. We'd have to be aware of being aware. How exasperating! Taking responsibility for all of our thoughts! So, not only would we have to be aware of our thoughts, but we'd also have to be aware that we were choosing them, including all the ones that seem to run away from us without our consent.

But letting our thoughts run on as if they have a mind of their own is an essential part of the thinking process. It's how we talk to ourselves; that's how everyone talks to themselves. It's just what we do. The things we say to ourselves are simply that, and, for the most part, we keep them that way because there are so many of them and because whatever is happening in our minds has no real bearing on anyone else. No one needs to know what we're thinking. It's not like it going to end up affecting them, and it's not going to affect us, either, because we can stop thinking whatever we're thinking any time we want.

Then how come we don't?

How come we don't stop telling ourselves the same things over and over again? You know: the things that keep us feeling downtrodden, defeated, betrayed, victimized, angry, hurt, ashamed, inferior, marginalized, discouraged, cheated, suspicious, worried, overwhelmed, self-conscious, nervous, and afraid?

No wonder at the end of most days we're so tired. These thoughts, these choices have exhausted us, and all the while we've been telling ourselves we have everything under control when actually, these conversations, the ones we unknowingly are having with ourselves, are controlling our lives. And they *are* conversations, just like the ones on these pages and the ones which have been controlling our lives since the very beginning. But since we've gotten so used to what they sound like, we seldom recognize that not only are we doing the talking and listening, but we're also not paying attention to how much these conversations are affecting us. All too often, whatever it is we're saying, we repeat again and again without stopping ourselves, yet we have almost no trouble stopping other people from overloading us with their repetition. After a while, especially if we don't like what they're saying, we just stop listening to their same old broken records, but for some reason, we almost never stop listening to our own. We just keep playing them over and over in our minds thinking we can stop any time we want, but unless we're paying attention, we almost never do.

Instead, we walk around wondering why we feel and act the way we do and make the choices we make. We wonder why we feel frustrated, unmotivated, misunderstood, unhappy, and most importantly, who made us feel this way?

Although we can and do come up with a wide variety of explanations, the only truthful answer to that most important question is always the same.

We did.

And we still do by underestimating the effect that our thoughts have on our lives. Perhaps we feel more accountable to our words and actions because they seem tangible and, therefore, memorable, whereas our thoughts seem rather harmless since we keep them to ourselves. As long as we don't share them with anyone, we can pretend they don't exist. As long as we don't act on them, they are of little consequence.

Right?

Well no, that isn't right because every one of our actions, words, and thoughts is preceded by an earlier thought that inspires it. Nothing we do, say, or think comes about until another thought leads us there. Regardless of how impulsively we act or speak at times, our thoughts are always a split second ahead directing us and serving as command central.

See, our thoughts are always in command, and maybe because we're so used to them being that way, we forget they are, and we forget they are commanding us. At times it's almost as if our thoughts are separate and distinct from what we think of as "us" as if a third party is directing them. They are telling us what to do, what to say, how to look, how to act, where to go, when to eat, who to trust, who to doubt, who to follow, what to watch, what to believe. And they're firing commands at such a rapid pace knowing we can keep up and that we almost never stop ourselves once we get going. The mighty locomotives powering our trains of thoughts just keep barreling full steam ahead down whichever tracks we send them, and for the most part, we send them down the same ones every day. So, the only way our thoughts can ever switch tracks is by us stepping in and pulling that switch lever to send us down a different one.

In other words, we have to start listening to what we're telling ourselves in order to know and then change what we're saying. Once we do, we'll start noticing patterns in our thoughts and how frequently we use these patterns to shape and distort our realities. We'll also start noticing how our realities begin to change when we change our thought patterns and how much more vested we feel when we take responsibility for the process.

Simply put: We are responsible for who we become. Even if we stubbornly cling to the idea that someone else was responsible, it really was us.

It always is.

And maybe that's the most redeeming part of it because knowing and then accepting we write the script, direct the set, and play the lead in who we become makes it so much easier for us to become something else, or something more. See, if we want to make something more of our lives, we must first make something more of our thoughts, and that means making a conscious effort to keep our thoughts traveling down tracks which actually take us where we want to end up. Otherwise, we'll just keep attempting to get to places with the wrong directions on how to get there and the wrong instructions on what to do if and when we arrive.

In other words, if we plan to get somewhere in life, our thoughts must match our plans. We can't just keep saying, "We want to be happy" while thinking thoughts that never feel happy or lead us to happiness. Just like we can't keep climbing the wall of worry every single day expecting to feel something other than worried at the end of the day.

But perhaps most importantly, we can't live our lives believing that other people are responsible for our thoughts because, by doing so, we will be allowing them to live a second life through our thoughts. Without even knowing it, our lives, the ones which supposedly belong to us, will end up being mostly about them.

There will always be other people peddling their viewpoints and telling us what to think, but the extent to which we accept what they tell us by converting it into what we tell ourselves is the only way they can ever influence us.

We are the gatekeepers of our thoughts. We are also their creators; we make them, sustain them, and have the power to change them, so why not treasure them by protecting ourselves from whomever and whatever we allow to occupy them?

Our thoughts make us who we are. Even though they often seem quite meaningless, they always lead us to the next one, but when we're racing through them, we rarely notice they are connected. We barely notice they are around.

But they are always around, which is why, if we let them, they will be our closest allies, just as we will be theirs. It will be through these alliances that we come to know ourselves.

It's simply a matter of switching tracks and choosing to live more consciously.

Epilogue

I hope you enjoyed reading this book as much as I enjoyed sharing it with you. At minimum, I hope it made you think. It certainly has made me think and, as I mentioned at the beginning of the book, it also has made me rethink a great many things, too.

Perhaps we both are striving to become more aware of our thoughts while becoming more aware that we are choosing them. What I've learned thus far is that reaching that level of awareness is going to take some time, so I just keep working at it day by day.

Part of that work includes creating a sequel to this book titled, "The Do-It-Yourself Sequel to Conscious Living: Repeating the Same Grade in the School of Hard Knocks". At this stage, I plan to include chapters on humility, patience, procrastination, perhaps even faith. Here are some sneak peeks from chapters to come:

A CHAPTER ON HUMILITY

Have you ever noticed the more you start feeling like a hotshot, the more you start thinking like a hot dog? We go from winner to wiener pretty quickly, often without noticing when this rather tricky transition takes place.

A CHAPTER ON PATIENCE

Most of us can relate to the feeling that, even if we're in a rush to go nowhere, we don't like being held up, and we don't like waiting, either. But if we continually structure our lives around never having to wait, won't the absence of never waiting lead to us forgetting the value of patience? In other words, if we don't have time for patience, and the essential component to patience is always time, won't we always end up with impatience?

Please keep an eye out for the sequel, as well as the soon-to-be released audio version of my first book.

Updates will be posted on my website: http://loriegivens.com

If you join my distribution list on my website, I'll gladly keep you posted on the release of the sequel, upcoming events, speaking engagements and book signings. It would be my great pleasure to thank you in person for welcoming my creations into your life.

Please follow me on Twitter: @loriegivens
LinkedIn: www.linkedin.com/in/loriegivens

Acknowledgements

There are several people I would like to acknowledge whose influence ultimately led to me writing this book.

To my late father, John V. Saviano, I offer a special tribute of gratitude for always providing your children with lots of tools to sharpen our minds and lots of material to sharpen our wits. ☺ Thank you for fostering in us a curiosity for learning along with the confidence to question conventional wisdom. I miss you, Dad.

I'd like to thank my mom, Elizabeth ("Bettie") Frazier, for staying at home to raise us when we were young and for shouldering a good bit of that responsibility alone because that's what being a military wife and mother demanded. Although you never framed it as such, your choice to forfeit what may have been your own dreams opened up a world of choices for each of your children. I love you, Mom. ☺

To my very special band of brothers, John, Jimmy, Jerry, and Jeff Saviano: I am so proud of all of you for growing into such fine men. Thank you, Johnny, for being our moral compass and for taking the role of firstborn as a responsibility to lead and look out for the rest of us. You always have done so without hesitation and without expecting anything in return. ☺ Thank you, Jimmy, for being my closest ally when we were young, and for letting me tag along (even though you didn't have to). You always knew just what to say to send me rolling on the floor in laughter. You still do. ☺ To my younger brother, Jerry: thank you for being the highly trained critical eye that I have imagined constantly as I wrote this book. Your talent as a writer has driven me to work much harder. I truly admire that you have used your accomplishments as a tenured Ph.D. and gifted literary expert to improve the lives of your students, especially the "forgotten" ones whose gifts are sometimes less apparent. ☺ And lastly, to my youngest brother Jeff: I continue to marvel at the immense capacity of your mind as well as your seemingly limitless desire for knowledge. Thank you for always being such a good listener and for sharing your viewpoints and ideas in such kind and unassuming ways. ☺

To my two very dear friends, Jeffrey Brian Worsley (1960-1993) and Martha Jo Nickey (1954-2016) who left the planet far, far too early: know that you each touched my life in such meaningfully memorable ways. I miss the sounds of your voices and laughter, as well as your steadfast friendship and wise counsel. I look forward to when we meet again.

A number of years ago as a young adult, I was fortunate to work with two remarkably impressive people whose examples would guide me through much of my career. One of those people was Ms. Nancy Thompson Oakley (I believe she now is known as Nancy Thompson Ham.) Nancy, thank you for teaching me that if something needed to be done, the best time to do it was "now". I attribute much of my desire to be productive in life to you. Another one of those people was Ms. Rebecca "Becky" Moon, who is still very much a part of my life today. Beck, it never ceases to amaze me how your grace, charm and good humor continually light up any room. You've taught me so much through the years. Thank you.

I also have a number of prior bosses and managers who were real stand-outs, so I'd like to include them in my acknowledgements: Mr. Stephen Gehret, Mr. Ronald "Ron" Bell, Mr. Ronald Leach, Mr. James Matarazzo, and Ms. NanEtte Epperson. Thank you all for having the wisdom to see that, in addition to a modest amount of well-placed support, some people simply need the freedom to succeed.

Thank you to my friend and physician, Dr. Corey Cameron, whose integrative approach to healing continually confirms that the body and mind work together to achieve complete wellness. Your insight and encouragement about this book have been very helpful.

Thank you to my long-time friend, Ms. Cindy Botelho. Somehow despite the many demands competing for your attention, you always find the time to let your friends know they matter. Thank you for always letting me know I matter. You are a wonderful friend.

Although it's been a long time, I'd like to acknowledge my high school English teacher, Ms. Linda Lee, for encouraging my love of writing.

I also extend a special thank you to Ms. Delisa Cobb and Mr. Randy Nance, two people who were once a part of my life, and to whom I will always carry debts of gratitude for their kindness and friendship.

To Ms. Kim O'Neill, I thank you for your vision, insightfulness, and generosity in sharing my work with your community of readers. Thank you to Dr. Elisa Medhus and her son, Erik, for their bravery and for inspiring me to think beyond my own limits.

Thank you to my capable copy editor, Ms. Alison J. McGuire from County Wicklow, Ireland, for identifying my writing tics and repetitions which ultimately led to some very helpful stylistic shifts. Perhaps more importantly though, thanks for letting me know that my book inspired some ah-ha moments within you. I was touched by your remarks.

Thank you to Ms. Tara Mayberry of TeaberryCreative.com for your beautiful book cover designs, expert formatting, and consistently exceeding my expectations. Thank you to Mr. Jarrett Holmes of Social Media Titans for your technical advice and artful contributions to my website, and thank you to "WengtheMeng" for your skillful video editing of my book promos.

I would be remiss if I didn't include a heartfelt thank you to my in-laws, Mr. Vincent and Mrs. Catherine Givens. You both are absolutely the loveliest people. It has been my great fortune to have been part of your family and to have been married to your son for so many years.

And finally, I offer my deepest gratitude to my husband, confidante and truest friend, Jim Givens. You are the genuine article, a self-made man, and the most well-rounded individual I have ever known. Your hard work always inspires me to work harder. Thank you for allowing me the space and freedom to write this book and for the many hours you spared listening to me narrate chapters. Your unconditional love, unwavering support, and boundless generosity are the foundation of my happiness.

Yes, there have been many people who, in one way or another, made it possible for me to write this book, far too many to mention for these purposes. The ones I've mentioned affected me in such favorable ways, but I also feel gratitude toward the ones whose effects were less favorable. Sometimes figuring out who we don't want to emulate in life is just as valuable as figuring out who we do. Good, bad or indifferent, everyone can teach us something.

In summary, I have pictured all of you in my thoughts as I wrote. Thinking back on our times together has brought to mind some very heartwarming memories. In one way or another, you all have inspired me to share my message with the world. For that and so much more, I thank you.

Some Things about Me

Although I was born in Georgia and lived in the Florida Panhandle until the age of six, I "grew up" in North Carolina, most of which occurred in the small town of Burlington. I was the middle child of five, flanked by a pair of brothers on each side.

My brothers were my first friends and a big part of my young life. So were my parents. Dad was career military, born in New Jersey from parents who had emigrated from Italy. Mom was a native North Carolinian who became a stay-at-home mom until my youngest brother completed his first few years of school. We were a working-class family, and as kids, we were expected to do our chores and anything else our parents decided needed doing. They kept a firm grip on us, at times quite literally with far more severity than necessary, but somehow we kids always managed to sneak laughter back into whatever it was we were supposed to be doing.

When chores and homework were done, we were allowed to play, and play we did, especially outdoors. Nothing could compare to the adventures we could drum up with other kids in the neighborhood.

Of course, everyone had a bicycle. That meant freedom, the very freedom that fed our desire to explore and test our own boundaries.

The TV was a big part of everybody's world back then, and for the most part, we all watched the same stuff. It was good stuff, too. There was Gilligan's Island, The Andy Griffith Show, Batman, Bewitched, Gunsmoke (Mom's favorite), The Munsters, Green Acres, the Beverly Hillbillies, and so many other now classics. In our house, the nightly news was a must. Even as kids we were expected to know about current events, so we watched the world through the eyes of Walter Cronkite, and yes, we watched the first Apollo lunar landing.

At least once a month on a Saturday morning, Dad would take us downtown to the Burlington public library, where he'd made sure we each had our own library card. We kids had the run of the place, although I don't think the librarians much cared for how eagerly Dad let us roam. I always hurried downstairs to the kids' section. It was quiet and, until my younger brothers came along, I mostly was the only kid down there. Dad let us each take home as many books as we could carry, and that's usually what I did because, with so many choices, I felt the only fair way to decide was to read them all.

My brothers and I all did well in school. It was expected and I guess, by watching each other as well as watching out for each other, we all bought into that expectation. We were lucky to have been raised in an environment that not only encouraged learning but also encouraged our curiosity to question what we learned. Plus, it was an added bonus to have older siblings on hand to help with the really tough homework. For me, that was Chemistry with Ms.

Betty Reynolds, the one teacher who could write and erase faster on a chalkboard than anyone I'd ever seen.

I've never really asked my brothers if they liked school as much as I did. If I had to choose, I'd say middle school and my senior year in high school were my favorites. My first two years of high school were the most awkward for me. Mostly that was because I had braces and constantly was dealing with those tiny rubber bands and that god-awful headgear, the latter of which I flatly refused to wear to school. My brother, Jimmy, occasionally (but good-naturedly) referred to me as "Braces Faces". Luckily he only did so at home. I was so happy when those braces came off. I remember the very next day shyly smiling during cheerleading practice before one of the other cheerleaders commented that she thought my teeth looked "big". (Yes, it was one of those kinds of comments that stay with you throughout your entire life.) In her defense though, on those rare occasions when I try on any shade of red lipstick, I do think I bear a striking resemblance to The Joker, particularly the one played by Cesar Romero.

In my senior year of high school, I changed schools which made it kind of difficult to have what you'd call a "best" friend, but I sure did meet some really nice kids. Since I had given up cheerleading in my junior year, I had to find other activities. So I entered the High School Pageant and ended up being chosen as first runner-up behind an amazingly talented girl who had as much stage presence as singing ability. A few weeks later I was offered the opportunity to choreograph all the dance numbers in the High School Musical, including my own which was for the part of a mute dancer who found her voice through falling in love with the leprechaun in Finian's Rainbow. It was a wonderful experience for all the kids who participated, including me for having been entrusted by an adult with such a big responsibility.

School and family played enormous roles in my young life. As did my teachers. I had some really good ones, and I feel fortunate to have grown up in a time when admiration and respect for the teaching profession were much more commonplace.

I entered college immediately after high school, and that was quite an awakening. The degree program I ultimately chose offered an interesting mix of economics and business classes. Although I had received a generous academic scholarship, my own personal economics necessitated that I work full-time, so I did by teaching exercise classes, selling fitness memberships and, after a short time, managing health clubs. It turned out to be a really good opportunity because I continued to teach exercise classes during evenings and weekends for the next twenty-five years and because it enabled me to meet some really wonderful people, including several close friends who are still in my life today.

I graduated college in 1983 from the University of North Carolina at Chapel Hill. (Yes, I went to school with the basketball legends, Michael Jordan and James Worthy, but I don't think they were aware of me. Oddly enough, I was asked about them in almost every job interview I ever had.) Soon after college, I began a full-time career as an entry-level financial operations manager with Roche Biomedical Laboratories (now LabCorp). Quite serendipitously, that first opportunity came from a woman who had purchased a fitness membership from me and had taken a few of my classes. She turned out to be a great boss.

Although I loved that job, as well as many of my co-workers and friends in North Carolina, I decided a couple years later it was time to move on. So I started targeting jobs along the eastern seaboard of the U.S. After a few months I accepted a similar job with a company based in Fort Lauderdale. I've lived and worked in various cities throughout Southeast Florida ever since.

Of the five siblings, I was the first to move outside of North Carolina, but eventually, all my brothers did the same. My oldest brother, Johnny (now "John") lives in Miami Beach; Jimmy is in Atlanta; Jerry is in Honolulu, and Jeff is in Las Vegas. Mom still lives in North Carolina. Dad retired to Hawaii where he died some years ago.

I didn't meet my husband, Jim, until 1995, so in the interest of brevity and out of respect for other people, suffice it to say that prior to meeting him I had a handful of failed romances. Although I used to make excuses for those failures, the truth is that I was the one choosing incompatible mates, especially ones I thought I could "fix". Fortunately for me and the other folks involved, I finally learned that the only thing I could fix, as well as the only thing that really needed fixing, was my desire to do so. After I had that epiphany, a few short weeks later, I met Jim. You guessed it, in one of my exercise classes.

Around that same time, I decided to make a professional transition from financial operations to sales, specifically selling complex financial products within the housing industry. This decision was a big one for me and also a really good one. Selling enables you to see the fruits of your labor in ways other professions do not. During these years, I met and worked with some incredibly talented people, including many amazing customers from all over the world. I think, because I found the work so gratifying, I was able to achieve a number of professional accolades. The most memorable to me was ranking as the top national producer out of 642 sales reps in a Fortune 500 company's annual sales contest. As proud as I was of the accomplishment though, the timing turned out to be somewhat bittersweet. The award ceremony that year was held in Hawaii, just a few days before I was to visit Dad's gravesite for the very first time. (Other than my husband, no one was aware of the overlapping events.) The award included a trophy, along with many kind words and humbling praise, but it also included a commemorative lei of Hawaiian Kukui nuts which I respectfully left behind on Dad's gravestone in remembrance of his life.

It wasn't long afterwards that the financial crisis struck and brought devastating chaos with it. Given the devastation, I ultimately decided it was time for me to move on, and I left feeling fully intent on assisting the hardest working guy I know, my husband, grow the family business he single-handedly had created. Although happy to assist, I unknowingly and quietly began to slip down a deep dark hole of my own making. Choosing to believe that my purpose and professional identity had been taken from me made the hole even deeper.

That's the hole that inspired me to write this book.

As you know, it is my first book.

It hasn't been easy, but I suspect reinventing oneself seldom is.

The good news is that through writing this book, I found my way out of that hole, and I did so by focusing less on the "things" I had done and more on the person I had become. That's why I've chosen to include some things about myself in this "About Me" section that sound less like a resume and more like a conversation with an old friend.

In some ways, I believe I owe it to you.

How could I write a book about mindsets and self-awareness without taking a few minutes to reveal some of my own? Especially ones that require me to step outside my comfort zone and speak to aspects of myself that I've never really shared with anyone, including a few of the circumstances and decisions in my life which likely influenced me far more than anything I could ever put on a resume. I share them now to demonstrate how much at any given moment we keep in our heads that no one else really knows. And yes, oftentimes it's because no one else has ever asked or even knows to ask, but they are examples of the kinds of conversations we have in our heads that ultimately become the mindsets which pilot our lives.

See, through the awarenesses I discovered while writing this book, I stopped looking at myself through the singular lens of my "background" and my "work", and I began looking at the real work that was needed in order for me to really see myself.

So now having written such a book, I would feel somewhat disingenuous trying to pose as some sort of subject matter expert while knowing that my entire objective was to demonstrate that the only way to become a subject matter expert on your own self-awareness is by doing it yourself.

Look, I'm as guilty as the next guy when it comes to making up reasons not to listen to someone before I even consider what they may have to say. You know the feeling, "Why should I listen to *them*? Who are they to tell *me* what to think?" Honestly, it's just what we do. We throw around our credentials, backgrounds, status, and class distinctions secretly hoping to one-up one another while simultaneously espousing the need to end a class warfare we continually promote. I can only imagine how much good advice and wisdom I have missed out on in my life because I chose to prejudge other people before I even listened.

As I told you in the Introduction, the focus of this book would not be about me or my mostly unremarkable life story because, in my opinion, it is far more remarkable to line up our stories alongside each other and witness our collective similarities when it comes to looking at ourselves. Regardless of the professions we choose, our personal histories, or our particular stations in life, when we look at ourselves we each choose whatever it is we see, as well as whatever it is we show others.

In closing, I hope in some way this do-it-yourself guide and my willingness to share some things about me have put you at ease with some things about you.

Thank you for reading this book. If it touched you in a way that is worth passing on, please share a copy of it with a friend, and please post a review on Amazon.

Until next time with warmest regards,

Lorie ☺

Made in the USA
Columbia, SC
03 December 2018